# Fake News:
# Western Media's Fabricated Reporting on China

Maxime Vivas

Prunus Press USA

This edition is published by Prunus Press USA.

**Fake News: Western Media's Fabricated Reporting on China**

Written by Maxime Vivas

First Edition 2023
ISBN: 978-1-61612-154-9

Prunus Press USA

# Contents

# Preface

One evening in September 2015, I was dining with some friends in a taverna in Athens at the invitation of the Ambassador of Venezuela, whom I had known in Paris when he was just an embassy attaché. A few streets away, in the year 640 BC, Solon was born, one of the Seven Sages of Ancient Greece, a statesman, a legislator and a poet, venerated by Xenophon, Plato and Aristotle. In the West, he is said to be the father of democracy. He abolished part of the private and public debt and debt slavery for the first time in the world, putting the interests of the people before those of the individual. When someone asked him, "Master, tell us what is the best political system?" He replied, "Tell me first where, in which country, and at what time."

The French system, which had been in place until 1962, and was considered by the French, our allies and our media to be democratic, saw the President of the Republic elected by the Parliament. Charles De Gaulle modified the Constitution so that the President was then elected by direct universal suffrage. Everyone considered that this revised procedure was completely democratic, in any case much more so than the previous one had been.

Therefore, the countries of the world which lacked the foresight to modify their presidential election systems when we did, seemed to us to live under questionable democratic regimes — inferior to our own. In the eyes of the world, during the time of the system of the Fifth Republic, we were enjoying a modern and almost democratic Constitution, but our exemplary Constitution was modified twenty-four times after 1962, the year when it was admirable to us and worthy of being adopted everywhere and by those countries which claimed to be democratic.

Of course, according to our "experts", in order to enjoy our congratulations and the label of "democratic country", these countries would have to be attentive to the constitutional changes taking place in France. The result of such changes is that out of the original ninety-two articles of the 1962 Constitution, only thirty still exist. It is not without irony that I point out here that Solon was right to say that democracy can vary according to times and circumstances. The French political system has been so changeable over time that we cannot reasonably judge democracy in other countries in relation to our own Constitution, which is perfectly unstable. Yet this is in fact what our media and most of our politicians do.

# The Rarely-known China

The great sociologist Pierre Bourdieu who wrote a lot about our media, developed a concept that he called "the Circular Circulation of Information" which can be summarized as follows: a newspaper or a news agency releases information; the media companies read each other; information published for the first time is then taken up by other media, without verification; and the validity and veracity of the information come from its repetition throughout the media. The ubiquity of initially unverified, but everywhere repeated, information is such that politicians repeat it too. The media then quotes the politicians and the seeming truthfulness of the initial information is reinforced. The information is no longer contestable. Anyone who tries to verify it and eventually claims that it is false will be labeled a conspirator, a negationist, or a propagandist. The status of journalists will unanimously be awarded to those who have spread erroneous information, while the person who has actually performed journalistic duties by not spreading lies with political connotation, will be seen as an activist. This is what happened to me when I told the truth about

Xinjiang. In such a context, the French, European and Western public in general has a backward looking vision of China which is fixated on the China of several decades ago.

The first time I came to China was in 2008, shortly before the Olympic Games. I was visiting one of my sons who was then living in Beijing. Just so my reader understands what I am about to say — and so that I may be forgiven — I must qualify that I am French, born in France, but that my parents were Spaniards. Quite naturally, I was interested in Spanish speaking countries which shared Spanish culture, such as those in Latin America, and Cuba and Venezuela in particular, two countries which I have visited several times and on which I have written books and many articles. I did not know a great deal about China. That is to say, I had a caricatural and truncated vision of it, the vision fabricated by our media. That vision is colored by people dressed in overalls with Mao collars, working 18 hours a day, sitting on the ground, eating rice with chopsticks on the dirty streets of the countryside or in gray towns whose avenues are heavily criss-crossed by bicycles lacking brakes. I don't need to tell what I actually saw. You know the true situation is much better than I thought. However, most of my compatriots ignore it.

In 2008, I visited Beijing and Xi'an with its Terracotta Army as a tourist attraction. In Tibet in 2010,

I visited several villages and towns including Lhasa and Gyantse. I also visited other cities, the most important of which were Urumqi and Kashgar during my two trips to Xinjiang in 2016 and 2018. Between 2008 and 2018 I saw the speed at which China was developing. Between those two visits, I was able to observe Xinjiang's forward march as it gets itself away from poverty. Please note that I am not hoping to paint a picture of heaven on earth. I am neither blind nor naive. I write in the hope to counter the incredible mountain of lies being poured out on China under all manners of pretexts.

The time has come to stop saying that China is "the world's factory" just because labor here, referred to in the West as skilled, is cheap. China is no longer cheap and is much more skilled now. The time has come to see that technology transfer (the sale of patents and products) is no longer a West to China one-way street. The time has come for Chinese research to file patents for the West to buy. The time has come for the West to have another look at China, a curious, lucid look, without the distorting ideological lens.

If you ask a passer-by on a street in Paris, "Do you know that 9-year-old Chinese children work 12 hours a day to make Huawei phones?", the chances are, he'll sympathetically say, "Yeah, it's awful." You will get the same kind of response if you talk about Uyghurs or Tibetans. "Yes, it's awful." You can perform this experiment in any city or town in France and you will have the same results. You will get these results in most Western countries. How is such ignorance of the truth possible? It is possible because of a weapon that the Americans are the only ones to master, a weapon equipped with tens of thousands of ideological warheads and launching bases in dozens of countries. That weapon is propaganda. Americans are the world champions in the art of launching fake news that will fly around the planet, refueling in tabloid newsrooms, radio stations, and television channels so that it may travel even further and penetrate millions of brains.

Initially, the so-called Uyghur affair was only the flutter of the wing of a butterfly which had not aroused much attention; however, then it was secretely hoped that, this flutter would trigger, from the USA, a global storm clouds to mass around China. Its variation was the vial brandished by Colin Powell at the UN[1] to frighten the Atlanticist world (which considers itself to be "the international community").

It becomes an international campaign, a rumor bellowed by websites, newspapers, radios, televisions, politicians, sinologists, researchers, experts, specialists:

---

1. On February 5, 2003, Colin Powell, George Bush's Secretary of State, told the UN that Iraq had weapons of mass destruction. Duped by the CIA, he now laments that his advocacy of war to the United Nations is "a stain on his reputation". Iraq was destroyed and there were hundreds of thousands of deaths.

the jostling cabal of plotters and rascals. In France, all the details have been presented in such a way as to provoke the indignation of our Marianne[2] in the Phrygian cap. However this fake news smacks of the CIA.

None of this is surprising thought. The fact that throughout almost all of Western world, all of the mainstream (Atlanticist) media, the so-called "humanitarian" associations, parties and numerous Internet sites have all taken up this rumor without the slightest effort at verification, and this gigantic piece of fake news is immediately transformed, de facto, into universal truth.

The dominant ideas are those of the ruling class, said Marx. For the Western world, history is written in Washington. Not in Beijing.

The France of the Revolution of 1789, where the *Declaration of the Rights of Man and of the Citizen* was signed, should however rather rejoice at the idea that the sway of the United States over dozens of countries will be reduced — the reduction of its power and therefore of its virtual impunity.

France is not in competition with China in the first place. We have no interest in making China our enemy.

---

2. Here it refers to the French people — Editor's note.

The United States has launched a global propaganda offensive to try to curb China's advance and possibly even prepare the world public opinion for a military adventure. Trump said "America first", his successor, Joe Biden, said, the very day after his election, that the United States is ready to lead the world. President Xi Jinping speaks of development "for a community with a shared future". It's a very different goal. The Belt and Road Initiative worries the Americans a great deal. The European Union, as it usually does, therefore walks in America's footsteps. It is ridiculous because, if the supremacy of the United States is threatened by this pharaonic project, Europe can benefit greatly.

Before this media tsunami began, most French people had never heard of Xinjiang. They now know the word "Uyghur" which is for them synonymous with the word "victim". They may be unlikely to confuse Uyghurs with the word for yoghurts as Bernard Kouchner, Sarkozy's Socialist Minister of Foreign Affairs, did. However, they still ignore, and perhaps always will, the name of the capital of this region, which is three times the size of France, or one-sixth the area of China (with its president whose name remains largely unknown in France). In spite of this, many of my compatriots are still ready to sign the "Free Uighurs" petition. It is fair to say that this anti-China campaign is rooted in one particular reality: the uniqueness of Xinjiang Uygur Autonomous

Region with its large Muslim population, and influenced by a long porous border with Pakistan (a doorway to Daesh).

The region has been a hotbed for terrorism which has seen several hundred people killed across the country and as far away as Beijing. The Chinese authorities apply a rigorous policy against what they call "the Three Evils" (fundamentalism, terrorism, separatism). Though the Uyghurs benefit from favorable measures ("positive discrimination" in terms of education, the creation of businesses), Xinjiang is the subject of meticulous and constant surveillance to prevent renewed murderous attacks.

Beijing's bet is that by reducing poverty among the Uyghurs, by developing education, by containing religion within its religious limits, Xinjiang will keep peace and become a non-problematic region, without anyone having to give up their language, their culture and their beliefs.

The global disinformation campaign is aimed to persuade us that Beijing had chosen the cudgel, an act which would, if it were at all true, represent the height of stupidity and ignorance, given that this method has been used a thousand times around the world throughout the ages and has everywhere failed.

Despite its aggressiveness, the political-media campaign against China's policy in Xinjiang only has the effectiveness of a mosquito bite on an elephant. The goal of the campaign is not to help the Uyghurs in Xinjiang.

The aim is not to protect the lives of the Uyghurs. The aim is to create unrest in the territory of a country that has awakened and is advancing peacefully towards the global pole position. At the same time, it is the objective of preparing world opinion for any muscular American measure so that Trump's country retains its leadership.When I talk with French journalists and reproach them for spreading such lies which fuel hatred of the Chinese and a kind of racism in France, they reject the charge, saying "Mr. Vivas, you are mixing up unverified information that is circulating on social networks on the Internet, and propagated by the will of anonymous liars, with the work of real journalists of the mainstream press". It is true that some of the accusations which I gave a partial list above on are the prerogative of propagators of lies on the Internet. But I also object to the above assessment of these French journalists.

The mainstream press never denies the large number of anti-Chinese lies about the situation of the Uyghurs. They never denounce the crudest lies. They pretend they don't exist. As if they had somehow reached the French mass but skipped the eyes and ears of journalists. How could this be then? Its answer is that these crass, unbelievable lies, boundless in imagination and horror, lay the groundwork for their own lies and their campaigns to smear China. At a push, we might say that the mere suggestion from our honorable media, our state media, our private media subsidized by advertising and by financial aid from the state, is lacking in credibility.

Then, over the months, the following phenomenon occurs. When it appears that genocide, concentration camps, torture and execution camps, organ harvesting, prove to be lies so crude that they can no longer be supported, and when personalities, indisputable intellectuals refute them, it is then that our media discreetly backtracks without admitting that it has lied. I was talking a few months ago with a journalist from *Liberation* whom I have already spoken about here. I blamed his newspaper for writing on its front page cover in huge letters: "Uyghurs genocide in progress". I said to her, "You know very well that it's not true." (She knows this since she was a specialist in this region where the population is increasing.) "The last great genocide that we experienced was the Jewish genocide in Europe and you know that at the end of the Second World War there were 6 million fewer Jews. That's genocide, that's the will to exterminate a people". She replied by saying, "Ah, but did you read the article in the inside pages? Because we made the distinction between genocide as you define it, and genocide as described in an article of the Geneva Convention of 1948 which specifies that there is genocide if measures are taken to limit fertilization, procreation".

We can see that this answer is the beginning of a retreat, yet one which is hypocritical since the title of *Liberation*, even if this newspaper has a small circulation, is visible in front of all the newspaper kiosks, on all the advertising posters for the newspaper. Moreover, if one wanted to waste time ranting about the definition of genocide by the Geneva Convention one could say that the one-child policy which affected the Han, and also all the "Family Planning" organizations (regulation and birth control) around the world represent a kind of genocide.

Let's continue my conversation with this reporter. I reproach her newspaper for having spread the monstrous fable of the removal of deadly organs from children. She exclaims, "Oh no, we never talked about that!" Unfortunately for her, I'm not asserting anything that I'm not sure of. I kept a copy of a page from *Liberation* which alerts its readers against this organ harvesting and which launches a petition for it to stop.

What remains of the accusations on this subject? The concentration camps. My interlocutor refuses to use the word "concentration". She prefers the term "internment center". It is possible that to Chinese readers there is no great semantic difference. But it's something else for the French because the concentration camps were extermination camps built in Germany by the Nazis and in which many French resistance fighters, mainly

Communists, and many Jews perished. And finally my interlocutor confides to me that she does not accept the number of 1 million, 2 million, 3 million "interned" Uyghurs. For her there are maybe 200,000 to 300,000.

Well, what are the sources then? One is Mrs. Gay McDougall. This American is a member of an independent (private) organization, CERD, which works for the UN on the issue of the elimination of racial discrimination. The organization is not a member of the UN and its staff are not employees either. Without having investigated or set foot in the field, without being able to provide the slightest scrap of evidence, Mrs. Gay McDougall, affirms that (not CERD) "credible reports" (which she does not produce) informed her of the mass detentions of millions of Uyghurs in internment camps. Immediately, Reuters, without carrying out the slightest verification, without having seen one of these ghostly "credible reports", relays the information, attributing it to the UN. The unsubstantiated allegations of a US citizen become an indisputable UN report. However as the veil is still a little thin, Reuters calls for the help of a human rights agency in China, whose headquarters is in the United States and which is subsidized by the United States government. Reuters does not consider it useful to give these details. Two references are therefore necessary: the UN and human rights defenders. The next reference comes from Human Rights Watch, an

American organization whose biases are constant and patent[3]. Then come the established press organs, the *New York Times*, the *Wall Street Journal*, the *Financial Times*, the radio stations directly financed by the CIA (Radio Free Asia, Voice of America…), researchers, sinologists, experts who read the press, all alerted by "credible reports", and motivated by their past work and their aversion to China.

In France, there is an odd character who is very active on the Web. Here he writes "Route de la Soie", elsewhere, on his Mediapart blog he writes "Silk Road", which is proof of his playfulness. His writings are a treat for anyone who wants to study the methods of disinformation.

Let's have a look at some of his work. "Xinjiang is widely cited as one of the most heavily controlled places[…] ". Who says so? "Human rights groups[…] " Which? "Alarming reports of an internment system[…] ". Which reports, and written by whom? "According to a significant number of credible reports, a United Nations panel of experts". No comment. "A Uyghur man said[…] A Uyghur who escaped told us[…] Some sources allege torture[…] Ten Uyghur exiles confirm[…]". He then cheerfully quotes the *Financial Times*, the *Washington*

3. See https://www.legrandsoir.info/l-ong-human-rights-watch-est-elle-trop-alignee-avec-la-politique-etrangere-des-etats-unis.html  https://www.youtube.com/watch?v=DPt-zXn05ac

*Post*, the *Wall Street Journal*, Associated Press, all bodies exhilarated by the possible revelations in "UN reports", an unreal starting point for a journalistic toast that they will back up with their archives and with testimonies from Uyghurs whose names will not be given to protect them and their families. A real pantomime! They read each other, copy each other, compete with each other, ever more enthusiastic, ever more sure.

The number of lies I have seen these days about Xinjiang (where I was) is such that it would take weeks to counter all of them.

And that's what they want, that we go after the bait that they lay. (And I find myself doing just that!) When the mountain of lies has crumbled, they will lay another bait, boosted by their media cronies. One malevolent invention follows another, and as long as there is always, one lie at play, the plan is working.

The worst is that, because illusion has been taken up everywhere (with pleasant variants and imaginative additions), whoever dares to dispute it, falls into the drawer labeled "ideologists", "campists", etc. In the case of China, the labels of "Maoist" or "friend of dictators" are vogue. It is a pleasant thing for me to stand up for the truth about China. I never had the slightest affinity with the Marxist-Leninist Communist Party of France (PCMLF). I subscribe to the curious profession of the non-faith of Jean-Luc Mélenchon. I also subscribe to the *Munich Charter*, known as the *Journalists' Charter*, which so many of my colleagues have either not read or forgotten, or which they voluntarily betray, but still wonder when faced with the subsequent opprobrium of the readership.

What's happening in Xinjiang?

On my left, the Chinese government and its pharaonic project for a new silk road that starts in Xinjiang, annoy the USA beyond belief.

On my right, the USA, its clandestine CIA, fanatical Islamists, terrorists, Uyghur separatists. All Uyghurs? Certainly not! But all are concerned, involved in spite of themselves by the tense climate, by the multiplication of surveillance devices.

In the fight that is being waged in Xinjiang, the worst results of which could be the separation of this region from China and the installation of a theocratic regime, the Chinese authorities are acting without weakness, I repeat.

They have clearly designated "the three scourges" and they will not suffer terrorism, the threat of their territory to be amputated, or any possibility of the fools of Allah laying their bloody fists on 21 million Chinese in Xinjiang (who are not all Uyghurs and Muslims). Of course, together with the USA, Europe gives lessons to the Chinese on how it should behave. Europe, not only rejects all Beijing's offers for collaboration in the fight against terrorism, but also denies that hundreds of Chinese victims of attacks were killed in the name of Allah and by emulators of Daesh. In an attack on a police station on August 4, 2008, 16 Chinese people were dead. On October 28, 2013, in the attack on the Tiananmen Square in Beijing, 5 were dead and 40 were injured. On March 1, 2014 in the attack at Kunming station (the capital of Yunnan province), 29 were stabbed to death and 130 were injured. However, this unanimity of the criticism of China, on all subjects, always, only has the tangible result of demonstrating our allegiance and platonic solidarity with Uncle Sam in its fight to maintain leadership over the world. "America First!" Hardly a year goes by without Uncle Sam massacring a people (preferably distant and weak) and stealing their resources.

America's fight is not ours.

We are not arguing with China for pole position. We have no interest in making an enemy of it. Our remonstrances have even less impact on the Asian giant as we lecture on subjects where our expertise remains to be demonstrated.

We have failed in many ways. We have failed by allowing poverty to develop, by creating ghetto neighborhoods, and again by grouping individuals in prison who will become "radicalized" inside. Another way we have failed has been our bombing of countries in the Middle East that have done nothing to us. In the background, China is dramatically reducing poverty, creating schools and mixed-population settlements. It keeps its soldiers at home and, as Li Xiaojun explains "sets up vocational training centers, educational centers".

In the 1900s, France deployed hussars throughout its territory. The hussars were teachers whose mission was to wrest education from the hands of the Church, to fight superstition, and to carry out everywhere the values of the Republic, one and indivisible. They were projected to the four corners of the department, there to fight against ignorance, to glorify the Republic, and to keep the hat on their head throughout their processions as Marcel Pagnol pleasantly described in *The Glory of My Dad*. In dozens of closed places called schools, millions of malleable young brains have undergone an education that has contributed to making the France of today, a unified hexagon freed from the Vatican. From where I sit, I can hear the eternal and unstoppable "China and France's situations are not the same!" Perhaps the time, the place, the stage of development and environment are indeed different. However, the fight is one and the same.

The hussars of the Republic worked to appease conflicts by ensuring the coexistence of contrary opinions.

This is what the authorities in Beijing and those of Xinjiang Uygur Autonomous Region are working on now. The Chinese leaders will facilitate the peaceful coexistence of ethnic groups, promote education, and lift Xinjiang out of poverty and certain economic backwardness.

To properly assess the nature of communications from the United States, it is best to refer to the words of Mike Pompeo, the former United States Secretary of State, from a speech to students from Texas A&M University on April 15, 2019. Reminiscing about his experience as Director of the CIA from 2017 to 2018, he confessed, "We lied, we cheated, we stole." And with a frankness that many French journalists envied, he added: "We had entire training courses [for it]".[4]

In the video, we see Mike Pompeo as he makes this statement. He laughs, visibly pleased with himself. What is scary is that we hear the students laughing too. An important figure in the political life of their country boasts of having lied, cheated, stolen and young people laugh. When the America of yesterday recounts its dishonest actions, the America of tomorrow expresses

---

4. See https://www.youtube.com/watch?v=DPt-zXn05ac

its satisfaction. But, if you think about it, this video has an even darker aspect. The footage was filmed, and Pompeo knew of that. The video was then released by the conference organizers. It was not about secret confidences delivered in a closed place and intended for reliable accomplices who will be able to keep quiet. No, everyone assumed that all over the world people would rejoice in his deeds alike, as if they amounted to some harmless minor prank: lying, cheating, stealing.

I took the risk writing a book telling the truth about Xinjiang, in the midst of a media storm of lies, an international storm with its origins in the United States of America. I don't take pride in it. Certain circumstances and particularly trips to China, including two trips to Xinjiang qualified me for this and made it my duty. I sort of played the role of an intruder, who walks into a lecture theatre where all the scholars and bishops are hunched over a flat table on which they have laid the flat map of the flat earth. They admire the flatness of the planet which, for them, is indisputable. Its flatness is a truth that has been known for centuries upon centuries. Then the intruder approaches them holding a globe in his hand. A few centuries ago, such an intruder who dares to offend science and God might have been burned. In the France of 2021 and 2022, the terrible power of such bishops and scholars is no longer as great, and the lives of their opponents are safer. Or so I hope.

# The West Is Flooded with American-style Propaganda

A person who suffers from bipolar disorder expresses their emotions with excessive intensity. They can experience events with deep sadness or a feeling of extreme happiness.

For some examples of the above we might consider the late Madeleine Albright.

She remained impassive while watching the destruction of Iraq on TV, but she tore her hair out when Russia brutally pushed back the NATO nuclear missile installation which is 5 minutes from Moscow.

She coldly stated that, "The death of 500,000 Iraqi children was worth it", but she cried continuously on BFM when she learned that a bomb had killed a blonde girl with blue eyes[5].

If such examples of bipolar disorder were properly addressed, 90% of Western media would be on medical treatment.

---

5. See https://www.youtube.com/watch?v=CYrPvRk0j-8

Chinua Achebe, a famous Nigerian author, quoted the great proverb —Until the lions have their own historians, the history of the hunt will always glorify the hunter. There's a sentence from the film *Howard Zinn: A People's History of the United States* — As long as rabbits have no historians, history will be written by the hunters. In his book *A People's History of the United States*, Howard Zinn demonstrates that history is written by the victors. And up to now, the winners of the media war are in Washington, not Beijing. At the end of the 15th century, there were an estimated 9 to 11.5 million Indians in North America, but no more than 250,000 in 1890. What kind of magic could transform such a genocide into a cowboy epic? Why, propaganda of course!

After World War II, when a battered and crumbling Europe needed to be rebuilt, the United States lent money in the form of the Marshall Plan. It was economic aid, but this plan included binding clauses, instruments of indoctrination in favor of the American way of life. Such clauses stipulated that 30% of films screened each year in our cinemas be shot in Hollywood and dubbed in French. That is the reason the French adore the "friendly" cowboys, the same cowboys who exterminated the Indians to seize their land.

Contrary to what they say, French citizens aren't bad at Geography. They can tell you where Alabama, Dakota,

Texas, California, Nevada, Florida, Pennsylvania, North Carolina, Arkansas, Arizona, Ohio, Oklahoma, Tennessee, Kentucky, Kansas, Colorado, New Hampshire, Minnesota, Michigan are situated. Yes, few are our compatriots who have never heard of the fifty states that make up the USA. Now, let's move on to the most populous country in the world and see how many Chinese regions our French compatriots can name. They can cite four of them, that is, those which our media invite us to watch: Tibet, Hong Kong, Taiwan, Xinjiang.

In terms of European history, the brainwashing is such that a majority of French people are unaware today that the Nazi army suffered a terrible defeat between July 1942 and February 1943 in Stalingrad from which it did not recover. Propaganda makes them believe that it was American soldiers who defeated Hitler with the Normandy Landings on June 6, 1944. It wants us to forget that on May 2, 1945 Berlin was conquered by the Red Army and that the scarlet flag that was planted on top of the Reichstag was decorated with a hammer and sickle. American troops did not enter the city until two months later, on July 4, 1945.

In France today, it is difficult to speak calmly, serenely, of the development of China[6], of the

---

6. See Annex 1

extraordinary changes taking place there in its economy, in culture, science, technology, education, town planning, ecology, and the rights of its citizens. This virtual impossibility of having an objective, neutral, calm, scientific, historical, sociological, anthropological (which I might summarize as an intelligent) dialogue on China results in impoverished thinking and analysis, and therefore general stupidity in our media.

André Malraux, General de Gaulle's Minister of Culture was a great writer and an expert on China. His novel *La Condition Humaine* about the Chinese Revolution won the Goncourt Prize. In his book *Les Conquérants* (Gallimard, 1947) he writes " China is China, and the rest of the world is the rest of the world". China is China because of its centuries-old civilization, its multi-ethnicity, and because of its time-honored culture, that is to say, because of what is common to its people, the thing that binds them together, and what they have learned, produced, invented and sometimes developed alone, by the means of their own genius, and what makes them far different from other peoples who shaped their own culture according to the vicissitudes of their history, wars of conquest, and invasions. France, a nation with a history of war has fought with almost all of its neighbors, conquered and occupied part of Europe with Napoleon, colonized peoples on all continents, and suffered occupation by neighboring countries, such as England or Germany. France's cultural identity is imbued with that of others. Centuries of occupation by the Romans disrupted the culture of Gaul. This reminds us of Spain, which was occupied for 700 years by the Arabs. And then, when peace reigned, there were peaceful, desired, solicited exchanges in the fields of art, music, architecture, and philosophy. In 1515, Francis I of France met a polymath painter in Italy, a veritable renaissance man, who was simultaneously an artist, scientist, engineer, inventor, anatomist, sculptor, architect, town planner, botanist, musician, philosopher and writer. Francis brought him to France, offering him a castle. The Italian was Leonardo da Vinci whose most famous work *The Mona Lisa* is admired at the Louvre Museum in Paris by tourists who come from every corner of the earth. What I mean to say here, is that my country is a mosaic of different cultures (there are hardly any French people who do not have a foreign ancestor) and that we are essentially no different from most other Western peoples. We have the same handwriting, and we do no eat with chopsticks.

As for China, and even if this country had never been closed off from the rest of the world, even if it had never experienced autarky, in many respects, its history and its geography have made it a different country. Its intrinsic particularities are engraved in its physical and cultural DNA, which distinguish it from the other peoples of the world.

Now, this brings me back to my point, that is, the impossibility of having an objective, neutral, peaceful, scientific, historical, sociological, anthropological dialogue on China as we have on other countries has led people to attribute Chinese characteristics which are cultural, customary, ancestral to the Communist Party of China and to its decisions, characteristics which, even if they surprise us and seem debatable to us, had existed before the birth of the People's Republic of China, before the creation of the word "communist", and before the concept of communism existed. And they will persist no matter what.

There are, in the nature of the Chinese, in their relationship with the authority, in their conception of democracy, of justice, of their attachment to public service, things that we cannot understand, especially because we don't discuss them. Therefore, we tend to misunderstand China and the Chinese people, and this misunderstanding is an obstacle to brotherhood, and to the mutual enrichment of cultural exchanges. Surely, it is high time for the French, in the reciprocal interest of our two countries, to tear themselves away from geopolitical illiteracy which induces economic blindness and a certain freezing of human relations.

The United States has determined to slow down China's progress, continues to explore the various means it has at its disposal to achieve this aim. Opening a war against China is very risky, even suicidal. A trade war, with a system of sanctions, taxes, etc. presents the risk of identical countermeasures. A propaganda war is effective but it is useless if it is not followed by the concrete offensives that it would necessarily lead to. Among the concrete measures which are currently being considered by the strategists of the United States of America are those which consist in weakening, dividing the Communist Party of China, and the Chinese government. Despite all its qualities, and perhaps because of its sheer size of 95 million members, the Communist Party of China must take care to perfect, improve, and renew itself, to preserve its cohesion and discipline, and to strengthen its union with the people. And indeed it does. If we consider what happened to the Soviet Union, we see that it did not disappear after an armed imperialist attack, nor did it fall because of a counter-revolution, an uprising of the people. It disintegrated from the inside out and from the top down, in a state of dazed indifference to the people. With regard to China, the United States of America hopes that such a scenario will repeat itself. I am convinced that they will be frustrated. I see that they have been trying this method for more than 60 years against Cuba and without success.

The United States still has the weapon of destabilization and disruption to use against China. When it came to Tibet, they lost. In Hong Kong too, it seems. There remains Taiwan, and then Xinjiang, a region three times the size of France, which represents a sixth of the China's territory. It is also a starting point of China's new silk road. I have been studying this issue since 2016, since I first travelled to Xinjiang, a journey which I discuss in my book *Uyghurs: Putting an End to the Fake News*.

Yet, I remember back in the 2010s, Western brainwashing was terrible. One evening, I had a dozen guests at my table and the conversation came to Tibet. They wanted to know what I had seen. I showed books illustrated with magnificent photos, and I answered the questions, and played Tibetan music — so strange to Western ears — in the background. However, my friends, who are educated people (most of them are college or high school teachers), had a hard time believing me. Me! Their friend, a man who they know doesn't lie was contradicting what they had learned from the media. They tended to object to anything that I said that was the bare truth. After a while, annoyed and feeling mischievous, I added, "The most amazing thing is the levitating monks!" All the guests suddenly gave me their attention. No one told me they doubted it, on the grounds that it was clearly impossible, as the laws of physics prove. One of those present, a history teacher, asked me hopefully, "Really?"

"No", I said, "That's in Tintin in Tibet". Monks cannot levitate air. Nobody can.

This anecdote shows us the extent to which propaganda has penetrated French minds. We can believe the worst lies, the legends, and refute the truths if our media tell us to.

Mandela, a black lawyer in South Africa, languished for 27 years in prison. In the Battle of Cuito Cuanavale in January 1988, Cuban and Angolan soldiers looted the South African army. On February 11, 1990, Mandela was released. On July 26, 1991, Mandela traveled to Cuba to publicly express his gratitude and to tell the crowd that, without the help of the Cubans, he would still be in prison. On May 10, 1994, at the age of 76, he was elected President of the Republic of South Africa. Soon after, he also travelled to China to thank the nation for having always supported and helped him.

Eminent personalities from all over the world attended the funeral of Nelson Mandela on December 15, 2013. Some were simply guests, others were invited to give speeches and this was the case of Chinese Vice President Li Yuanchao, Special Representative of President Xi Jinping. Other personalities were not invited despite wishing to. Among them was the Dalai Lama, who had not been able to obtain a visa despite the insistence of petitions of Archbishop of Johannesburg, Desmond Tutu on his behalf. In France, political commentators were indignant at the absence of the Dalai Lama, and the fact that Raul Castro had been authorized to speak in front of the coffin, while President François Hollande and former President Nicolas Sarkozy had not. The Dalai Lama, persona non grata, had to content himself with expressing "his sadness at having lost a dear friend" from a distance.

Dear readers, I ask for your full attention here. During Nelson Mandela's 27 years of imprisonment, the Dalai Lama remained silent. He did not intervene once. But when, in October 1998, the former Chilean dictator Augusto Pinochet was arrested by the British police on the basis of an international arrest warrant for crimes against humanity, the Dalai Lama reacted very quickly to demand his release[7].

I have published many articles to help my readers discover the real China. In 2011, I wrote the book *Behind the Smile: The Hidden Side of the Dalai Lama* in which I revealed what Tibet was like before its liberation in 1951. It has been translated into 6 languages.

In December 2020, I wrote the book *Uyghurs: Putting an End to the Fake News* in which I detailed what

---

7. See the book, Maxime Vivas, *Behind the Smile: The Hidden Side of the Dalai Lama*, Translated by Lisa Molle Troyer, Long River Press, 2012.

I saw during my two trips to Xinjiang in 2016 and 2018. It has been translated into 13 languages. This book came up against a backlash of Western propaganda, leading to insults, threats, false articles, and extreme defamatory accusations. In spite of such malicious and trying volleys, as numerous as they were repetitive, I was elated and proud when China's Minister of Foreign Affairs, Mr. Wang Yi recommended my book be read at an international press conference on March 7, 2021. Shortly after, I received the "Special Book Award of China" in September 2021 for my contribution to the promotion of cultural exchange.

In France it was a different story. I was the target of the private and public media who never gave me a chance to defend my position. Their method is to multiply their trials in the absence of the accused. In matters of justice there is a principle immortalized in the Latin expression "audi alteram partem" which means "the need to hear the other party". It refers to the right to be able to present one's version of the facts during a trial before being judged. This right exists in the justice system, but not in the trial by media. A trial in which you, the accused, do not have the right to speak, in which you are prohibited from using a lawyer, and in which all the witnesses are only there to prosecute against you, is of course unthinkable.

Between September and October 2021, IRSEM (the Strategic Research Institute of the Military School), a branch of the French army, published a report titled *Chinese Influence Operations: A Machiavellian Moment*, a 654-page[8] sinophobic report, and the result of 2 years of work. A glance at the report's contents is enough to reveal its purpose. It is a textual weapon in which China is caricatured and presented in such a way that it will be hated and feared. It also appears that this document, written in French and English, was primarily designed to be read by NATO military personnel and by the politicians and generals in the United States. It is an act of allegiance to the White House and the Pentagon. It is an accumulation of lies and trickery aimed to convince the readers that China is evil and that it is preparing to take over the world.

The IRSEM report quotes me fifty-four times.[9] That's more than it quotes Trump and Biden! The report also posts my picture eight times. It reminds one of the "wanted dead or alive?" posters of spaghetti Western movies. The report reveals that I was a trade unionist at the CGT (Confédération Générale du Travail), that I

---

8. See https://www.irsem.fr/rapport.html
https://drive.google.com/file/d/1yW8DZCDp9_6ZHoBN0zeR2CiZlTfjNZ2P/view
English : https://drive.google.com/file/d/1J_6CANw8xxn9pUWezHgwL83hH0jwIvs_/view

9. The English report quotes me sixty-one times.

was the literary referent of ATTAC (Association pour une taxation des transactions financières pour l'aide aux citoyens), that I supported the Bolivarian revolution of Hugo Chavez, that I dedicated a novel, the plot of which takes place in Caracas to the Fête de l'Humanité in Paris, that I host a cultural program on a radio station that was created by the CGT union forty years ago, that I am close to Jean-Luc Mélenchon, a French politician who was one candidate in the 2022[10] presidential election and who is also a friend of China. Such a character description is not frightening to anyone in France. At home, we see in this portrait a man who has lasting convictions and a commitment to the left. Nothing out of the ordinary. I am neither an anarchist, planting bombs and for the destruction of the state, nor am I a nihilist leftist. I have been threatened with lawsuits several times by my adversaries, but they have never materialized. I respect the law and if I have ever been penalized by the police for a traffic violation, I have paid my fine.

In the United States however, IRSEM's characterization paints me as a dangerous individual. In fact, seven of my books[11] are readily available to Joe Biden in the

---

10. The first round of the presidential elections (April 10, 2022) saw Jean-Luc Mélenchon take third place, just behind Marine Le Pen. French electoral law dictates that only the first and second place candidates can continue onto the second round.

11. See https://id.loc.gov/authorities/names/n99032025.html

extremism section of the Library of Congress. And that's why our army's anti-Chinese report quotes me so often, making me out to be some kind of boogeyman. To the report authors I am a Frenchman who, not only does not fit into an anti-Chinese discourse, but who is able to frighten Americans by virtue of my political stance. All this is perfectly legal in France, even common, but it is nonetheless shocking for the soldiers of the Pentagon, of NATO, of the Republican Party and of the Democratic Party who alternately occupy the offices of the White House.

This military pamphlet, which occupied a team of researchers for two years, is a sinophobic cancer that has spread to our army. The Military Research Institute wants the United States to know that the message has been received, and they do know that because among IRSEM's associate researchers we see a lieutenant colonel of the United States army who is in charge of liaison with NATO.

Under such circumstances, and at a time when France's resources are used to denigrate China, it is difficult to open our compatriots' eyes to China's realities. Such realities and the changes at the amazing speed call for our admiration.

# China Experiencing a Development with Crazy but Controllable Acceleration

My Cuban friends once received help from their big brother nation, the Soviet Union. The USSR did a lot for Cuba in the face of the aggressiveness of its neighbor, the United States. Cuba owes a lot to the Soviet Union, and perhaps even its survival. The truth is that the Soviets constructed buildings on the island which were similar to those they were building in the eastern European countries, which had been devastated by the war against the Nazis. People had to be housed, and quickly. We saw buildings began to appear that looked like huge matchboxes or gray parallelograms, which lacked both charm and imagination and clashed with the admirable Cuban architecture. Such buildings were also built in France after the war, because it was a necessity. We could house thousands of poor French people there. We called them "bars". The official name was HLM (Habitations à Loyer Modéré). Today, they have all been destroyed or demolished. However, buildings of the same style, but smaller, are being built in France today. When we look at the beauty of old buildings in our cities, we wonder what is going on. This is the law of profit. We must build at the lowest price to ensure the maximum profit for the developers.

I don't know how it works in China, who makes the decision and who issues building permits, but one thing struck me in particular. It was the great diversity, great fantasy, architectural audacity that I saw wherever I went. One is left with the impression that the decision makers want to build a more beautiful China. It seems that the beauty of the towns and villages is a form of progress offered to the people. This really caught my attention because many Westerners think that in China everything is decided by the Communist Party, and the government meticulously decides the rights, obligations and standards of the people. It's easy to make such an assumption because when it comes to the real estate, that's how we do things in France. In our country, government departments set the rules and make the choices. These are not entrusted to aesthetes, designers or artists. Most of the time, it is the elected officials in the municipality, in the department, or in the region, who have the authority to choose model projects when they have no competence in the related fields.

Does the reader know the story of the painter who asked a cobbler for advice?

In 77 AD, Pliny the Elder shared this story with us. A shoemaker pointed out to the painter Apelles an error in his representation of a sandal in a picture he was painting. The painter immediately corrected his work. Encouraged, the cobbler began to make further remarks about other things he considered to be mistakes in the painting. Annoyed, the painter replied, "Ne supra crepidam sutor iudicaret" (A shoemaker should not judge beyond the shoe). You have to stay within your area of expertise.

The elect are rarely elected for their artistic tastes. We must let the innovators and designers, that is, those who carry out surprising projects, express themselves, because they are new and exhibit a kind of madness. When I use the word madness here, I do not mean it in any pejorative sense. Madness can be a synonymous with audacity. Madness means immense imagination and know-how that unfolds in all directions, freely, and sometimes with great fantasy and humor. I have often seen this in modern Chinese architecture. I am thinking in particular of the most well-known avant-garde of Beijing's towers, the headquarters of the nation's central television network, which was built by a German architect with a team of Chinese engineers and workers and is in fact the second largest office building in the world after the Pentagon. Thanks to its shape and the appearance of its facade, the inhabitants of Beijing have mischievously nicknamed the building the "Pants". I open a parenthesis here to note again the cultural differences between the

French and the Chinese. In 2018 I was in Beijing with my partner. My friend, the Chinese journalist Zheng Ruolin, who I will talk about again later, had invited us to attend a show at the "Pants".

Understandably, security check there is strict. To get to the studio, we had to pass several checkpoints where my Chinese friend was required to present his identification. At one point my friend said to us, "I hope that with advances in facial recognition I will one day be recognized once and for all when I enter this building." You should know that in France facial recognition technology met strong opposition and is considered to be a setback for democracy and individual freedom which, for the French, require a certain degree of anonymity. A few days ago a friend sent me an email titled, "A Chinese store. Terrifying!" There is a video about a Chinese store, perhaps experimental, where a shopper is leaving a store in which there is no checkout. Outside the shop, the shopper shows us the screen of his smartphone where we can see the total of his purchases, and that his bank account has already been debited. Facial recognition makes it possible to identify the customer, and surveillance cameras record purchases. I imagine that in China, making things so much simpler is appreciated, but not here, at least not today.

When I mentioned control earlier, I did not only mean in terms of purchases, but in the overall life of the country. Such is the Communist Party of China, a young centenarian, that helps China advance coherently towards a defined goal which is a higher standard of living and knowledge, never before achieved in the nation's multi-millennial history. The Communist Party of China has designed and is developing a theoretical system of socialism with Chinese characteristics, a sinicization of Marxism that has enabled the most spectacular social transformation in the history of this once poor and weak country. The ideological choice made by China has surprised those who forget that a tree should be judged by the size of its fruits.

China has made the transition from a feudal regime, into a centralized planned economy, and then to a socialist market economy. The idea of a socialist market economy sounds paradoxical. It is nevertheless a Chinese reality — a new and audacious concept that will allow China to move from isolationism or semi-isolationism to an all-out openness to the rest of the world. This is how in only a few decades China has become the world's second economic power. Misery and famine remain only in the memories of the oldest Chinese people. Today the goal is to achieve a moderately prosperous society, but I believe that goal has been achieved already.

In the book published in 1973, *When China Wakes up the World Will Tremble*, the French writer, former diplomat, minister of culture and member of the French Academy Alain Peyrefitte wrote, "Before 1949, China was a country from the Middle Ages [...] a swarm of beggars with stumps, children covered with wounds, black pigs and lanky dogs; rags with the odd shred of brocade." When natural disasters occurred, famine swept everything away. The peasants were ruined immediately; when droughts and floods struck, they had no reserves.

General Secretary of the CPC Central Committee, Mr. Xi Jinping, has on several occasions spoken about the successes of the 100-year struggle of the Communist Party of China and the concept of socialism with Chinese characteristics with its socialist market economy, which is, in short, the sinicization of Marxism achieved by combining the fundamental principles of Marxism with Chinese reality and China's traditional culture, integrating the Mao Zedong Thought. This is the original product of the practice of Marxism-Leninism in China.

When President Xi Jinping speaks of success, the "concrete analysis of the concrete situation" proves him right. The Chinese economy has made a stunning leap forward. In just a few decades, China has successfully industrialized, a task that took developed countries several centuries to achieve. China has experienced the largest and most profound social transformation in its history. The independence of China and its advance in several fields, and on the scientific and technological level, have been affirmed. It has successfully transformed itself from a multi-millennial feudal autocracy into a democratic country of the people. Originally an overpopulated and poor country, China has become a socialist society which has put an end to famine and extreme poverty. Today, throughout China, the basic needs of the population are met.

This transformation leads to a change in China's relationship with the rest of the world. The page of history on which ancient China was subjected to abusive diplomacy has been turned forever. China is now in a position to proclaim that the days of being at the mercy of foreign powers which would humiliate it are over. China can no longer be humiliated, oppressed or enslaved by others. China has become a fully sovereign country with borders that it can defend, with a cultural and political stability which is favorable to the guidance of its own destiny.

The emergence of a new, prosperous, dynamic and optimistic China has only been possible due to the existence of a strong, united Communist Party which, since its founding, has always been faithful to its fundamental ideals of communism, which are the happiness of the people and the consideration of their interests, whether we like it or not, and whether or not the fact is accepted by the Western way of thinking,.

The Communist Party of China, conversely, since its founding in 1921, has remained faithful to its initial commitment to serving the Chinese people with the goal of reviving the Chinese nation. This is not the place to recount the history of China and that of the Communist Party of China in detail. However, there are visible, indisputable truths that demand our attention. China, once feudal, has shaken off its shackles. It has become the world's second largest economy even after a long period in which its productive forces had lagged behind. China has come to be strong and respected, after a period of weakness, and instances in which it was carved up by predatory states. This progress has been made in leaps and bounds.

At the end of 2019, during his usual Sunday school lesson at the Maranatha Baptist Church in his hometown of Plains, Georgia, Jimmy Carter revealed that he had recently spoken about China with President Donald Trump. He said Trump was worried about the growth of the Chinese economy and had expressed concern that "China is ahead of us".

Jimmy Carter replied by saying, "You're worried about China getting ahead of us, and I agree with you. But do you know why China is overtaking us?" "I normalized diplomatic relations with China in 1979. Since 1979, do you know how many times China has been at war with anybody? None. And we have stayed at war." The United States is the most warlike nation in the history of the world because it wants to impose American values on other countries. China, on the other hand, invests its resources in projects such as high-speed railways instead of devoting them to military expenditure. How many kilometers of high-speed railway do we have in this country? (Zero, replied the assembly of the faithful).

We have wasted $3 trillion in military spending. China has not wasted a penny on wars, and that is why it is ahead of us in almost every way. And if we had taken 3 trillion and put it into American infrastructure, we would have a high-speed railroad. We would have bridges that do not collapse. We would have roads that are maintained properly. Our education system would be as good as that of South Korea or Hong Kong (China)."

Jimmy Carter then reeled off the following figures, pointing out that 3,000 billion dollars were spent on Afghanistan and Iraq, and 70 billion on Syria, before adding, "Americans and government forces have killed more Afghan civilians than the Taliban."

Today's China is a powerful country moving towards prosperity.

China had already woken up when our media was still reporting that it was in hibernation.

# How Much Longer the West Could Hide a True China

To quote our great national poet Victor Hugo:

*Ils mordent les talons de qui marche en avant.*
*Ils sont humiliés d' aboyer, ne pouvant*
*Jusqu' au rugissement hausser leur petitesse…*

(Written on July 17, 1851)

One chapter in my book *Uyghurs: Putting an End to the Fake News* is titled "China walks ahead". China in the new era is beyond what we knew about.

China, which once lived in darkness, and which once bought patents, has jumped over our heads. Many of the world's patents are now Chinese. Over the past quarter of a century, China has lifted 635 million people out of extreme poverty (this is equivalent to the total population of sub-Saharan Africa). According to the website of Politics *People*, the number of destitute rural inhabitants decreased from 98.99 million at the end of 2012 to 5.51 million at the end of 2019. According to the Xinhua News Agency, the poverty rate had fallen from 97.5% in 1978 to 3.1% by the end of 2017. Over the past five years, one person has been lifted out of poverty every two seconds. Every two years, China produces as much cement as the United States has done over the course of the entire 20th century. It now produces as much steel as the rest of the world. Over a period of fifteen years, 20,000 kilometers of railway tracks were laid for high-speed trains, more than the total of the rest of the world. Over the past ten years, their average wages have tripled. With an increase of 10.5%, a rate well above the economic growth, the average wages in Chinese industry are now only 20% lower than those of Portugal. As of 2013, the minimum wages in Bulgaria, Macedonia, Romania, Moldova and Ukraine were lower than those in China.

China launched the world's first quantum science satellite. It synthesized synthetic chromosomes from chemical substances, and made the world's first quantum computer, capable of doing work that the world's most powerful computers would take a century to complete in just 0.01 seconds. China's first large airliner successfully undertook its maiden flight, and a successful test was carried out to generate power from flammable ice from the seabed. The high-speed Fuxing train reached the speed of 350 km/h, and pulsars were discovered through a giant telescope.

I have travelled to China four times, and I talk with Chinese people on the Internet. When a Westerner like myself speaks with Chinese people on the street or with journalists, writers, and political scientists, such a person might notice a feeling of a certainty in their interlocutors that we no longer have here in France. It is the confidence that life will be better tomorrow. In France, there are more and more poor people, social rights are called into question and people are pessimistic about their futures.

Seventy years ago, China was one of the poorest countries in the world. The per capita GNP was half that of Africa. Now in terms of its global GDP, China will soon be the leading economic power, ahead of the USA. In terms of its per capita GDP, the UN figures rank it the 90th (the USA is the 9th). It is clear that China is progressing at a spectacular rate, but it still has many steps to climb at home in order to reach the level of the great powers in the West.

I wonder how much longer the West can hide what China has achieved through its own genius, and through its economic successes which are back into its carefully conceived plans for development. I hesitate to give figures because I know that some are already out of date by the time I learn about them, and that they will therefore be even more obsolete by the time that this text is published and read. I will therefore remain cautiously evasive. China now has as many kilometers of high-speed railway as the rest of the world, around 40,000 kilometers. It has lifted roughly as many citizens out of extreme poverty as there are people in Africa. Famine and illiteracy now exist only in the memories of older Chinese people. Health care has made spectacular progress, infant mortality has fallen considerably while life expectancy has increased, and continues to increase. China has reduced world poverty by 70%, and 25% of world reforestation work between 2000 and 2017 was carried out by China.

Xinjiang's GDP has increased from over 900 billion yuan in 2014 to over 1.3 trillion yuan in 2019. Absolute poverty in Xinjiang has been eliminated, with over 3 million citizens lifted out of poverty.

Progress has reached the countryside in accordance with President Xi Jinping's mandate to create a moderately prosperous society. In Xinjiang, I was able to see this in small villages where you could still see mud houses, the doorways of which were so low that you had to bend down to enter. These houses were only there however as a reminder of what China was like in the past, serving as a foil to illustrate what it has become. Next to these houses were taller ones, identical in their secular style, but built with modern materials and large openings, benefiting from electricity, Internet, WiFi, household appliances and flatscreen TVs. What struck me was that the inhabitants of the old houses were not relocated miles away from what was undoubtedly their ancestral home.

The authorities had taken care not to uproot them. I imagine that this is not always possible everywhere, but I report what I have seen.

Some time ago, I had a Nigerian guest at my house. He explained one of his country's well-digging techniques to us. A few men from another province will dig manually, with a minimum of tools. They can find water up to 90 meters deep. Digging might take three months. There are machines in his country but using them is much more expensive than doing it manually. When I hear stories such as this, I understand why Africa is developing at such an exasperating snail's pace.

The USA is on the decline. Wounded animals are dangerous. With the Helms-Burton Act, America claims the power to decide who can trade with whom. Those who disobey are punished with fines. French companies and banks have been sanctioned accordingly and they paid up. Moreover, the US Army is the most powerful army the world has ever known. It absorbs as much money as the armies of half of all the other countries in the world. The US army is everywhere. It is close to China and Russia. It is therefore in China and Russia's interests to get along.

China is peacefully developing its Belt and Road Initiative, which links trade routes between China, Asia, Africa, Europe and Lain America. In 2020, 143 countries and 31 international organizations, that is, more than two thirds of the world's nations — these figures will no doubt be an understatement by the time that text is read — signed bilateral agreements with China as part of the Initiative. Partners include 19 Latin American countries among which we can mention Bolivia, Chile, Cuba, Ecuador, Guyana, Jamaica, Panama, Peru, the Dominican Republic, El Salvador, Suriname, Uruguay, Venezuela, Costa Rica as well as Trinidad and Tobago.

Barely a week after the November 2020 presidential elections in the United States and victory for Joe Biden, China signed the Regional Comprehensive Economic Partnership (RCEP) with 14 countries in the Asian-Pacific region, the most important trade agreement in the world. This agreement, which represents 30% of the world's GDP, involves more than two billion people and aims to create a gigantic free trade zone between China and the ten states of ASEAN (Association of Southeast Asian Nations), those being Myanmar, Brunei, Cambodia, Indonesia, Laos, Malaysia, the Philippines, Singapore, Thailand, Vietnam, as well as Australia, South Korea, Japan, and New Zealand.

The United States feels alone. I don't know why they cannot, little by little, cede a little of their authority. They could try to destroy China militarily, but the adventure could also be suicidal. On the economic level, the agreements made by China with most of the countries of the world reduce the United States' room to maneuver. Their technological supremacy is under attack. More and more patents filed around the world are now Chinese.

Pro-American Westerners, or at least their political and media "elite" will not admit China's spectacular progress. Since they cannot deny it, they hide it, they talk about it as little as possible and strive to multiply the criticisms and the accusations against China.

In November 2021 on the website Le Grand Soir, which I administrate, my friend Bruno Guigue, a professor of philosophy, a political scientist and once a senior civil servant — dismissed from his subprefect position over an article on Palestine — in response to those who say that China is imperialist asks[12], "If China is imperialist, why is it that 143 countries have agreed to cooperate with it in the Belt and Road Initiative? No one will deny that China is a rising power whose economic influence is growing at an unstoppable rate, but imperialism is something else altogether. This great country, which has not been at war for forty years, obviously uses other means to convince its partners to work together."

---

12. Imperialism and anti-imperialism. See http://lherminerouge.eklablog.com/imperialisme-et-anti-imperialisme-par-bruno-guigue-ic-fr-11-01-22-a211745312

With his permission, I want to quote Bruno again when he says that "China refuses to interfere in other countries' internal affairs and accepts no foreign interference in its own. Unlike Western countries, which claim to promote 'democracy' and 'human rights' through bombing campaigns, China believes that every nation must find its own way and that interference is a violation of international law. In short, it takes the Charter of the United Nations seriously and condemns the 'regime changes' enacted by Washington against any government which refuses to submit. Respectful of the sovereignty of other states, China cooperates in all areas with countries that wish to cooperate too, regardless of their political regime or their ideological orientation. This is how China works together with Venezuela and Colombia, or how it trades with Iran and Saudi Arabia. This is what President Xi Jinping calls the 'win-win' policy, in which everyone can find a benefit, and which respects the sovereignty of participating states. This policy is being implemented around the world. It is enjoying growing success in Asia, Africa and Latin America, that is, in the historic hunting grounds of the former colonial powers. With the Belt and Road Initiative, China exports manufactured goods and imports raw materials, before it monetizes its imports by building infrastructure. Beneficial for China, this program is also beneficial for partner countries. This is because it avoids repeating the mistakes of the neoliberal policies imposed by the West on developing countries. International institutions such as the International Monetary Fund (IMF) and the World Bank, in fact, require the implementation of austerity policies inspired by the Washington Consensus in return for their financial assistance. China does not demand anything. Clearly the BRI goes against the grain of the structural adjustment programs imposed by the IMF. Countries that want to work with China are not forced to privatize their state-owned enterprises, lower corporate taxes, or make deep cuts in social budgets. As China refrains from interfering in the internal affairs of other countries, it does not stake a claim in the guidance of the economic policy of other nations, rightly believing that this is the matter of national sovereignty. Certainly, China does not lend blindly and it preserves its interests. Its companies are sometimes greedy, and some projects are postponed as a result of persistent disagreements, but China respects the sovereignty of its partners."

Lenin defined imperialism as capitalism which has reached a stage of development in which the domination of monopolies and finance capital has asserted itself, where the export of capital has acquired a leading importance, where the division of the world between international trusts has begun and where the division of the entire territory of the globe between the largest capitalist countries has ended.

With this definition, we can see echoes of America's desire to lead the world, but we can also see how different this path is to China's vision, that of "a community with a shared future", which is to say a march towards progress and peace for the benefit of all countries, and not just one that would crush the others.

# The Politicization of Covid-19 and the Vaccine War

The Covid-19 pandemic has shown us several things. First, the European Union has no capacity or will to help its own people. Let us cast our minds back to a few years ago when Greece was undergoing a financial crisis, and let us remember how the European Union crushed it instead of helping. The Greeks had tasked Alexis Tsipras with the job of rejecting the austerity plans, renegotiating the debt. Europe however came together in the negotiations and Tsipras was humiliated. All concessions that were suggested were refused and the European Union demanded the continuation of policies which were unsustainable for the Greek people. Greece experienced a real tragedy, and its population was severely punished.

When Italy was for a time overwhelmed by Covid-19, the European Union was useless. It was Chinese equipment and Cuban doctors that came to the aid of the Italian medical teams. Even now, the nature of European policy makes a coordinated fight against the virus impossible. Each country does what it wants. On the other hand, where the European Union has been effective, it is in the multiplication of directives to member countries to reduce the number of hospital beds. In recent decades, there have been more than 60 repeated requests[13] from the European Union to member countries to remove beds. At home, Presidents Sarkozy, Hollande, Macron obeyed. The removal of beds has continued throughout the pandemic. The result is shocking.

When seeking to explain the successes of China, Vietnam, Cuba and Venezuela in their fights against Covid-19, our media propaganda has but one explanation: "Dictatorships!" How else can they justify their own ineptitude? The truth is that in these countries, a choice was made immediately between the economy and the people. China locked down an entire province, reducing all economic activity there to zero. Videos showing China building a hospital in 10 days were everywhere on our social networks. France, which lacked masks and resuscitation beds, allowed subways, crowded with workers to continue to operate. In Cuba, a country that I know and where I have friends, the government has bet everything on preserving the lives of its people. Cuba gave up its main resource, tourism. Cubans immediately made their own masks, often homemade and always free. The health system, known to be exemplary, has been magnificent. Cuban doctors who are very numerous went knocking on the doors of every house and building to

13. See https://www.humanite.fr/monde/union-europeenne/la-commission-europeenne-demande-63-fois-aux-etats-de-reduire-les-depenses-de

tell people how to protect themselves, taking people's temperatures and looking for symptoms. The population played the game, just as they were doing in China, and not out of a fear of the authorities, but out of a confidence in the guidance of their leaders and their doctors. On this Caribbean island, still subjected to an inhuman blockade, researchers have developed a vaccine while, in Pasteur's France, we are still waiting on ours.

And so to summarize, socialist management of the pandemic has proven itself to be successful. Capitalist management has its own hierarchy, in which the GDP, the banks and the economy are the most important, and people always come second. People are there to serve the economy whereas in a well-managed society it should be the other way round.

As soon as Covid-19 appeared in Wuhan, China in December 2019, the American propaganda machine fired up. In obeisance to that machine, media around the world, that is to say the Western world, began suggesting that China was withholding information, and that the authorities had tried to hide the problem leading to the World Health Organization (WHO) being informed late and the necessary measures at the global level being implemented too late. In truth, a careful and objective examination shows that the Chinese authorities reacted quickly, isolated the genome of the disease and released it to foreign specialists and the WHO. The precise origin was even speculated upon by our media: the virus was transmitted to humans by bats and by pangolins. Other hypotheses indicate that the Covid-19 virus was discovered in other places on the planet and at an earlier date, but they have been dismissed without further research and without further publicity.

The malady of untruth having been added to a pestilential situation, the next step was to profiteer. This is what was done with the Pfizer vaccine in particular, which has considerably enriched the American laboratory which manufactures and sells it by increasing its price over the months. Reputed by our media to be extraordinarily effective, this vaccine, first intended for the elderly, then for the youngest, then for all adults, then for adolescents, then for children, requires one injection, then two, then three. Today, we learn that it does not really protect against the disease, only serving to limit its severity, and that vaccinated people are contagious regardless. The observation that we can make right now is that we do not have a truly effective vaccine, not in the same way we do for the other diseases we treat or which protect us from them. At the same time, Chinese, Russian and Cuban vaccines are not authorized in France. Citizens who use them are not considered to be vaccinated and are subject to various limitations, such as not being allowed to go to a show, or to a restaurant. In the midst of this terrible disease, our rulers have started a vaccine war.

# The Rampage of French Media

In Xinjiang, in 2016, I travelled with around forty journalists from twenty different countries. I went back there in 2018 with my partner at the invitation of the local "Bingtuan", an army corps that manages part of the region's economy, which consists of far more than just agriculture. We crossed Xinjiang by plane and by bus. I didn't know the area at all before 2016.

I discovered a huge region, arid in parts, with deserts, mountains and a certain lag in development in the countryside. However, in the two years that separated my two trips, I saw progress, especially in rural housing. I also saw schools, modern factories, a pasta factory, a dairy production plant and a platform for buying and selling agricultural products, a factory that manufactures LEDs, filaments for screens, sensors, telephones and watches, a wind turbine factory, and a vineyard. Near the Aral Sea, we visited a huge petrochemical plant.

In 2016, along with other journalists, I met a 41-year-old Uyghur woman in Xinjiang, the head of a company that manufactures tracksuits. She told us that she had not been formally educated and the government helped her set up her business, which now employs 80 village women who are paid 1,500 yuan each month, and that her salary is 2,500 yuan, which — together with scholarships — helps her to pay for her son's studies abroad.

The possibilities that had been afforded to her and her son were so well received with such gratitude that tears of emotion came to her eyes as she told us her story.

Of all things that amazed me in Xinjiang, one episode in particular will forever be engraved in my memory. In a gymnasium on a land where the Islam is the first religion, I saw young Uyghur girls in leotards, holding on to the bar and throwing one leg over their head to music, and with no worry about my presence. I said to myself, if the authorities let fundamentalism win, young Uyghurs and other inhabitants of Xinjiang, whatever their ethnicity or their religion, would have to do without music, and without dance forever. They would have to hide their bodies.

I am often told that what I saw is just what they wanted me to see. I write about it in my book *Uyghurs: Putting an End to the Fake News*. I explain how, wherever you are in the world, when you arrive as a part of a delegation or an inspection team, you are always shown what your hosts want you to see. In a school, when the inspector arrives, everything must be cleaned, the teacher will be well dressed and the best students will be seated at the front. The Academy inspector knows it. Everyone knows it. I personally am a qualified European ergonomist. It used to be my job to analyze work places, to discover the difference between what I was told and what was actually being done. My job was to see what they don't show us and make improvements. I am quite experienced in this area and therefore, I know very well that we were shown what they wanted to show us. I saw what I saw. On top of this, when you visit a large number of establishments (factories, schools, farms), coherence will emerge. When we want to measure the level of sincerity, we can do it. We manage to get our interlocutors to talk, which is a kind of art of midwifery. I attended a large number of cultural performances, which were at times grandiose. So I say that in the Chinese regions I visited, the local culture is alive and beautiful. In France, our media tell us that it has been eradicated!

With regard to the language, the obstacle is the same for all journalists who visit foreign countries. We do not necessarily speak English in all countries. When I was in Tibet, China, with journalists from *Le Monde* and *Le Figaro*, we met people who spoke Tibetan. One may suspect that what was translated was not true. But when you really want to find something out, you can do.

I don't mind being told that I don't speak the Chinese language. It's true that danger exists in translation, and that translation is treachery as the Italians say. However, we can ask several questions, to several interlocutors, in several places to try to see when something is missing. There are hundreds of millions of people in the world who tell us what Christ apparently said, yet they do not speak Aramaic, the language of Jesus. Still, they report what he supposedly said! There are explorers who write books about tribes in the Amazon after having been there only once, without speaking a single word of the native language, and without an interpreter!

We know that China is setting up vocational training centres and educational centres. There are also prisons, just as there are in all countries of the world for the incarceration of common law offenders and for citizens who have committed terrorist acts or who threaten to do so. In my book, I detail the ferocity with which France once fought terrorism and separatism, and the harshness with which it fights political Islamists today. I also explain, without hiding anything, the methods used by China in the fight against "the three plagues" (terrorism, separatism, religious fundamentalism). It is not right, as our media often do, to embellish them.

I hesitated to write my book on the Uyghur people. I knew I would have to spend a lot of time writing it and

I was hard pressed to find a publisher for such a book. My worries proved to be well-founded. I gave up contacting most of publishers. Fortunately, a French intellectual, Sonia Bressler, a doctor of philosophy and epistemology knew Xinjiang well. She was appalled to see how it was talked about in France. She therefore founded La Route de la Soie Publishing House. She did so to ensure that there could be a space where the truth can be told about China. When I told her about my manuscript, she accepted it before she had even read it. She knew me by reputation and she understood what I had written. For more than two months, we read and reread the manuscript, considering even the slightest of details to ensure that it would not be accused of amateurism. The result was much as I had expected. It was not the book that was attacked, but the author and the publisher.

There are clashes on Facebook and Twitter about my book. The worst was with a very well-known online newspaper, the privately funded newspaper, *Arrêt Sur Images*. In February 2020, I gave a telephone interview to this paper. It turned out to be an ambush, a flurry of ad hominem, violent, rehashed, humiliating questions and accusations, intended to punish me for being a liar, naive; it was Reductio ad Hitlerum.

When one lie wears out, another arises. In the fall of 2021, we were told that "500, 000 Uyghurs are enslaved in the cotton fields." Suddenly, there was a campaign which urged consumers to boycott cotton clothes from China. The sad thing is that no journalist is willing to verify the information, no one wonders why there were not 500,000 slaves in the previous years or decades.

In detective novels, it is said that you have to find out who benefits from the crime. So who benefits from this rumor? If you go to the UN's website, and you look at its FAO (Food and Agriculture Organization) branch, you learn that the three main cotton-exporting countries in the world are the United States, India and China. The FAO foresees an overproduction of cotton in the coming years. The United States has an interest in eliminating a competitor. Our media are helping to do so.

Should complaints not be filed against liars who damage the interests of China and the Uyghur people? There are international laws against unfair practices that exclude competitors. They should probably be enforced, but on the other hand, journalists do not have the freedom to tell the truth very often, and must support the discourse which is guided by Washington.

I'm not going to elaborate on "unsustainable lies" here. Indeed, I am currently writing another text on the subject for the Chinese. However, I can quote the famous words of Antonio Gramsci as I consider this issue, "Telling the truth is a revolutionary act."

On March 31, 2021, at the height of the international media campaign against Xinjiang, the evening daily *Le Monde* which is considered the gold standard of newsprint published a scoop. The article purported to demonstrate that the Chinese foreign language news channel CGTN, which has a French language service, invented a reporter, and then quoted the individual claiming that the "information" presented by the French media about Xinjiang is in fact disinformation. Laurène Beaumond has indeed signed an article for CGTN, an article which will be immediately reported and promoted by the Chinese Embassy in France. But, for *Le Monde*, this journalist does not exist. Her name, Laurène Beaumond, is unknown to press professionals and she does not appear in the records of journalists who hold a press card. However, Laurène Beaumond claims to have lived in Xinjiang and to have married in its capital, Urumqi. The article she signed for CGTN gives a vision of this region that is different to that which is hammered out by our media. Quite frankly, she claims our media is lying and she does so with the authority of someone who has lived there and knows the area well.

The journalist from *Le Monde*, who was the first to launch the accusation about the non-existence of a very real French journalist, made three mistakes:

First, *Le Monde*'s journalist neglected to mention, or deliberately disregarded the fact that the possession of a press card is not necessary in France to enter the field of journalism. In fact, French journalists who hold a press card are a minority. Therefore, not appearing on the file of journalists holding a press card does not mean that one is not a journalist or that one does not exist.

Second, the use of pseudonyms in the press is a fairly widespread custom.

Third, the degree of duplicity and naivety which *Le Monde*'s journalist attributed to the Chinese is more commonly found in some French news outlets and among some French journalists. It is clear that the Chinese would be taking a considerable risk by inventing a journalist out of thin air, whose existence they would have been unable to prove. In fact, the journalist from *Le Monde* was a victim of her own pride and the self-intoxication that can be found in newsrooms in France.

I am very familiar with CGTN; they have interviewed me several times. I know the Chinese from the Chinese Embassy in France, including His Excellency Ambassador Lu Shaye with whom I had the honor of dining. I do not think for a single second that they would risk compromising themselves and their country with such a ruse.

At the end of a sloppy and superficial investigation, the journalist from *Le Monde* therefore thought she could affirm that the Chinese in Paris were liars. Such affirmations are quickly believed by our media, such is the strong sinophobic atmosphere. Of course, many media outlets have jumped on the information without having to take the time to verify it. A "researcher", Antoines Bondaz, a sinophobe expert, is a regular in our media, telling us we should think about China when coming to all the bad things. He decided that "Laurène Beaumond does not exist"[14].

The case was therefore made that the Chinese lie, that the Chinese manipulate information, that the Chinese only know propaganda.

Unfortunately for all these people, a few days later, one of the biggest French daily newspapers, *Le Figaro* actually met Laurène Beaumond, and on April 2, 2021,

---

14. See https://www.legrandsoir.info/antoine-bondaz-le-chasseur-deguise-en-chercheur.htmlhttps://www.legrandsoir.info/antoine-bondaz-le-chasseur-deguise-en-chercheur.html

they published an interview with her. It turned out Laurène Beaumond really did exist. She was not "invented" by a Chinese television channel, but Laurène Beaumond is not her real name, she prefers to use it as a pseudonym that protects her and her family from the hostility of our media when they write about China. She is right to do so. I speak from experience, having suffered what she wanted to avoid.

# Unavoidable Lies

The main industry in Toulouse, where I live, is aeronautics. It is the home of Airbus. This industry and dozens of subcontracting companies represent tens of thousands of jobs. The Chinese are our customers. In the largest bookstore in the city, one of the largest in France, the section devoted to China is quite small. Mine, is nowhere to be found. However, I am known in my city, and I appear in the dictionary of Toulouse personalities.

There is a brilliant young independent photo-journalist who I have known since he was a baby. I carried him on my lap, and his parents are my friends. He told me one day that he had to write an article on the Uyghur people. I warned him about the fake news campaign orchestrated by the United States and provided him with all the documentation I had on the subject. I thus hoped that this young man who held me in friendship and esteem, and who knows that I speak the truth, might distinguish himself from his colleagues. A few months later, it was his father, a little ashamed, who announced the publication of the article to me and told me about it. Nothing in the article was verifiable. In short, the work could not qualify as journalism. At first, I was very disappointed and, to tell the truth, a little hurt, on reading his report. Then I understood that if he had written an article using my documents, that is to say an article which told the truth and went against everything the press was writing, his article would have been rejected. Like many journalists in France, my young friend writes and sells articles to get by. The philosopher Émile Chartier wrote — I quote from memory — "When I see a young author arrive from the provinces with ambition and writing skills, I don't know what he will write, but I know what he will not write." My young friend travels the world with his camera. He has just obtained the prestigious diplomatic press prize for his work in India which will be awarded to him in the presence of the Minister of Foreign Affairs.

It's a well-deserved award and I'm happy for him. But I know that, if he had written his report on the Uyghurs using the documents that I had given him, not only would he not have this award, but his article would probably not have been published and he would be out of job.

Here I present a talented journalist. His mother, a friend of mine, is very involved in denouncing fake news about Cuba and works with me in the France-Cuba Association in Toulouse. Her son however co-produced a report with a section on Xinjiang adorned with inlays of bogus "satellite photos" and with a voiceover from beyond the grave for TV (Arte). The project was called "With the Global Security Act, we are taking another step forward in surveillance?" He was awarded the Albert-Londres prize, the most prestigious prize for an audiovisual work. And then there is the journalist from the daily *Liberation*, in charge of the Xinjiang file.

Let's see how, having to comment on my book (*Uyghurs: Putting an End to the Fake News*) after an interview that lasted 2 hours 30 minutes (30 minutes planned), a journalist from the daily *Liberation* put a target on my back. She even counted the number of times I have been quoted by Chinese "state media" (in France we refer to our own government funded media as "public media", such as France Inter, France culture, and France 2). So for 2 hours 30 minutes on the phone, we had a lively dialogue, and we argued. Then, after the interview finished, we chatted. What she did know about me already is what she had read in the press. She soon discovered that I was another man, a denigrated, slandered, caricatured, but honest journalist.

The day after the interview, she sent me an email, part of which I will present here. She asked me not to make it public. I complied with this request, even after the publication of the damaging and malicious article which she went on to publish in *Liberation*.

Her article stated: "In March, Qian He, director in France of the Chinese state-run website *People's Daily*, quoted Maxime Vivas on Twitter at least sixteen times, presenting him as a 'journalist' who conducted 'detailed investigations on Xinjiang'."

Notice I'm being discredited because *People's Daily* quotes me. In truth, I have written articles for French and foreign newspapers, I administer an information site which has selected and published 30,000 articles by more than 2,000 authors from all over the world, and I myself have written hundreds of articles on this site and on others.

Outside the interview, she told me that she had even investigated me with a journalist from *Le Figaro* (which is not mentioned in my book!). It is a curious step, which demonstrates that she was looking for arguments for an ad hominem attack. She told me that the *Figaro* journalist had said of me, "He's a nice guy." In the article published by *Liberation*, this assessment is somewhat different. "*Le Figaro* reporter, Renaud Girard, bumped into Vivas during a press trip to Tibet in 2010. On his return Maxime Vivas wrote a tirade against the Dalai Lama. Speaking on Viva, Girard said, "He was a friendly, down-to-earth guy from Toulouse, who thinks China is a tremendous success story. Does he have any ideological blinkers? Without a doubt."

Was it the blinkers then, that made Renaud Girard

want to stay in touch with me? In 2015 he sent me a copy of a book and with the message "Say, tell me, dear Maxime, what do you think of the book I just published with Régis Debray, *What's left of the West*?" I responded with a long review of the book.

The *Liberation* journalist had even checked the number of followers on my Twitter (I don't bother too much with it) and, seeing that I had a little fewer than her, deduced that I was a nobody. The number of books I have published (more than 20) have been translated into 13 languages, the literary prizes I have obtained, and the fact that seven of my books sit in the United States Library of Congress, within easy reach of the president might have nuanced her assessment.

Alas, this was a question of harming me, of diminishing me.

As the weeks went by, I found that her article was widely circulated on many networks. Worse still was the fact that when my name was typed in a search engine, her article appeared first.

So, considering that loyalty pacts should not allow everything from one partner and tie up the other, I published part of the friendly email she had sent me the day after our dialogue. The interview took place on March 17, 2021, her email the next day (the 18th), and her article is dated March 30, 2021. I published the email, in part, on

May 5 only. We measure my patience, my angelism in the face of a diabolically aggressive, contemptuous and too ubiquitous article on the Internet.

After a good month of loyal silence as one unshackling themselves, as one tearing off the gag from one's mouth, I published short fragments of the email I had received from the *Liberation* journalist:

"Dear Maxim, I hope you are doing well and were able to get some sleep after our verbal brawl yesterday. I actually went to bed and woke up quite upset by our conversation[…]. I am happy to have finally understood (finally, I think) the object of your fight, and to have been able to see the man and down-to-earth author behind the media figure. I found you to be a humanist, a lover of freedom, and culture. I understand that you are fighting to counter the falsities that we have read here and there on the removal of organs, extermination, the cremation of the living, and the banning of Uyghur[…]".

Here is my desperate conclusion. In such a media atmosphere in which the young son of my friend works, the same atmosphere in which the journalist from *Liberation* writes, it would be unrealistic to expect either to produce anything but that which they did.

In short, I have no anger. On the contrary I feel a sense of compassion. I am much freer than they are, and I can tell the truth about China with impunity. There remains though, the distressing obligation to return the compliment in order to discourage other potential aggressors. During the Franco-German war of 1870, on both sides of the trenches, soldiers were tearing each other apart at the behest of those at the rear, those in control of Berlin and Paris.

This is not the place to discuss sociological ideas, but we must nevertheless widen the field of reflection on the specific responsibilities of each journalist. These responsibilities exist and are determined by the place that each occupies in the media organization which employs him. The degree of freedom enjoyed by each journalist is not the same. The level of freedoms enjoyed by the simple "freelancer", the editor of a newspaper, the editor of a column on the radio, and a host-star of a television program are all different. We must interpolate the weight of the journalistic clan, the clan's propensity for solidarity, just as with any kind of clan, and the fact that journalists read each other and copy each other to eventually produce a monochromatic block of information that professes to be an indisputable truth (since no one disputes it). This is how global lies are spread. The sense of responsibility (and sometimes the good faith) of those who propagate such lies is diluted, carried by a current which seems as natural as that of a river. The logic, or the order of things, is to let yourself be carried away by the waves. Swimming against the current is dangerous, exhausting and even suicidal.

When one of my sons lived in Beijing between 2007 and 2008, he told me that the sky was always gray and that he couldn't see the sun or the end of the avenues because of a kind of fog, a thick mist that is called smog in English, which is actually a mixture of air pollutants that limits visibility in the atmosphere. During my last visit to Beijing in September 2018, the weather was beautiful, the sky was blue and the sun was shining. I'm not saying it's always like this in Beijing. What I'm saying is that great efforts have been made to reduce pollution, and these efforts have been successful. When our media talk about world pollution, they often point out that China is the biggest polluter. This information would be more accurate if it were supplemented the other important fact that China is the most populous country. However, when considering the pollution per inhabitant and, if we are in fact alarmed by the gigatonnes of $CO_2$ released into the atmosphere, we might note that Qatar, Kuwait, the United Arab Emirates and the United States of America are much bigger polluters than China.

In China, I saw major infrastructure projects, the fight against the advance of the desert, and the high level of ecological awareness (electric scooters, solar street lamps, wind turbine manufacturing plants, etc.). I have seen signs of the Chinese authorities taking ecological issues very seriously. The China of today attaches more importance than the China of yesteryear to the protection of ecosystems and the environment. The Chinese government, if I understand correctly, advocates for not merely seeking short-term economic growth and sacrificing the quality of the environment, that is to say, the mountains, rivers, forests, farmlands, lakes, steppes and sandy deserts. China's survival is at stake, a survival that necessarily involves a kind of harmony, a balance between development and the conservation of the vitally important environment. The fight against pollution is not simply a question of well-being and comfort, but a question of the utmost importance for the country, and China knows it.

I have seen in the *Resolution of the CPC Central Committee on the Major Achievements and Historical Experience of the Party over the Past Century*, adopted on November 11, 2021, that strict and detailed measures are being advocated. In Chapter 9, "Spurring ecological advancement", environmental protection is presented as one of the perennial pillars of the Chinese nation. The decisive battle against pollution is to be carried out according to the plan to combat air, water and soil pollution under the "blue skies, clear waters, clean land" campaign with a ban henceforth on importing waste from abroad for recycling. These are not only good resolutions alone, or lip service for the meetings, but effective measures with controls on the ground and sanctions ready to be implemented against those breaking the rules. If I seem to dwell on the subject of pollution in China and on the means of combating it, it is because I expect very much that similar policies could be adopted in my own country, and the issue of the survival of the planet could become more than just a subject of political speeches and news reports at the Conference of the Parties (COP) and the United Nations Conference on Climate Change.

On September 14, 2018, I left Xinjiang with my partner, but before flying to France, I made an appointment one morning to meet with the Chinese journalist Zheng Ruolin in Beijing, whom I knew when he was stationed in Paris as a correspondent for several Chinese media outlets. He helped me understand and love China. We got on well and, before his final return to China, I made a trip from Toulouse, where I live, to Paris without the time to have lunch with him. This time Zheng Ruolin wanted to ask me for a thirty-minute interview while we were in Beijing for the TV channel, CGTN, which broadcasts in French. He hosts the program "They Don't Tell Us Everything".

I have often recounted these reunions, and will do so again, because, in a political sense, they were significant, unforgettable moments with regard to the excess of French misinformation on China, and on the negation of China's efforts and its progress. This time we were going to talk about pollution. In Xinjiang, I had visited a wind turbine factory, I had seen kilometers and kilometers of solar panels along certain roads, and I had appreciated, as I mentioned above, the village streetlights that were powered by small propellers and small solar panels. I was happy to see the Uyghur people moving around on electromobiles. For the record, I was a municipal councilor in a village near Toulouse, and during my time in office I had failed to install a solar street lamp near houses that we had just renovated. The municipality preferred to install electric streetlights to illuminate a parking lot. What I had just seen in Xinjiang had particularly interested me and I dreamed of seeing villages in France take inspiration from it.

Zheng Ruolin came to pick us up at our hotel in the morning, an hour ahead of the scheduled meeting. He could not wait to show us something. It was a video, recorded on his tablet PC. We saw Nicolas Hulot interviewed in February 2015 by Jean-Jacques Bourdin on the television channel BFMTV-RMC for the program "Bourdin direct".

Nicolas Hulot, a well-known ecologist in France and also the Minister of Ecology, has hosted television programs. As for Jean-Jacques Bourdin, he was the host of a very popular television program.

Here is an excerpt from the dialogue that revolted my friend Zheng Ruolin.

Nicolas Hulot: "Someone said to me the other day when I was in China, that Chinese children do not know what a blue sky looks like, so saturated is China with pollution".

Jean-Jacques Bourdin, astonished: "Chinese children don't know... !?"

Nicolas Hulot: "— they do not know that the sky is blue because of the pollution...".

Here, I will summarize the final lie (well brought off by the host) of a well-established environmentalist who was Macron's minister: "In China, children do not know that the sky is blue". The "[...]in the cities" qualification of the original claim disappeared in the exchange that followed.

In short, from a truth (the fact of pollution in Beijing and other cities) a lie is invented that no one will denounce. No one, not even me, whose niggling vigilance over journalistic fake news had been taken for granted.

"Chinese children don't know the sky is blue." Hulot had said that he was in China "the other day". He had therefore been able to see that what someone had told him was false and that Bourdin, for whom the sun is hidden throughout China, added to this lie.

Zheng Ruolin, concluded tragically, and with a tone of pessimism: "In France, lies about China are never denied. They go around in circles in the media and become truth, without any reservations, by dint of their being repeated."

An astute observation indeed. When it comes to China, there is no risk in lying. Not a single voice was raised in France in the media to correct the Hulot-Bourdin double act which plunged us into the smog of misinformation by erasing the sun over an area of Asia 9,596,961 km$^2$ in size.

During the show on CGTN, I wanted to make a distinction between myself and Hulot and Bourdin. I felt obliged as my friend had been affected by their lie. I had to show people that France is not populated by 66 million hostile plotters.

# Only an Impartial Observer to See a True China

After my journalistic study trip to Tibet, China, in 2010, I kept in touch with journalist Renaud Girard, a great reporter in one of the most important French daily newspapers, *Le Figaro*. In 2014 he wrote a book entitled *What Remains of the West*. The book is a dialogue between Régis Debray and himself. Writer and philosopher, Régis Debray was a member of the Goncourt Academy. In his youth he was a companion of Che Guevara in Bolivia, where he was arrested and tortured. To give a quick anecdote, he was president of a jury for a literary grand prize where one of my books was in the running (*The Hidden Face of Reporters Without Borders*, in which I reveal the true face of this fake NGO and unmask its President, Robert Ménard, a great enemy of China). I did not get the prize. I had also written to Régis Debray that I didn't want it.

Renaud Girard, sent me a copy of the book he'd written with Régis Debray. Here I will quote a few passages. For Régis Debray, "the West has been able to represent its particular interests as the interests of humanity good and proper". Claiming to be "the international community", it is capable, with or without the approval of the UN, of overthrowing regimes placed at the antipodes, and regimes which do not threaten it, with the use of arms. Compare this behavior with China, which has never bombed a country "ten thousand kilometers from its coast", and with Iran, which does not encircle the United States with "air, land and naval bases located on the borders of Mexico and Canada". Worse still, "the US defense budget equals that of all other countries combined…". "Only NATO has bases on five continents (which include eight hundred American installations abroad."[15]) Huddled in between are Europe —"light of the world", and France — "teacher of the human race". For Debray, American power is so intrinsically strong that it tolerates and digests opposing ideas. It knows how to "mythridatize itself by a regular absorption of critical negativity". "They thought police are stricter in France."

Here I would like to point out that the political system in the United States stems from a history of conquest over an immense territory achieved through the violence of settlers who came mainly from Europe. It is marked by individualism and the supremacy of particular interests over the general interest. Such state of mind

---

15. What Remains of the West? Régis Debray et Renaud Girard, Grasset, 2014 https://www.legrandsoir.info/que-reste-t-il-de-l-occident.html

is consolidated by a powerful media system. And this is why we see, in every presidential election in the United States, two major parties clash. The Republican Party, which is anti-communist and in favor of waging wars everywhere, and the Democratic Party, which is pro-capitalist and an opponent of peace. It is just as the leader of the Communist Party of France Jacques Duclos once said at home when speaking of two French right-wing politicians: "It's six one, and half a dozen of the other." In fact there is a joke which goes the American political system, with the election to the presidency of a candidate from the Republican Party, or from the Democratic Party, is like buying a hot dog. The Republican might want ketchup, the Democrat is keen on mustard, but it's always the same sausage.

Back to Régis Debray. By evoking the superiority of the United States in terms of scientific and technical innovation, Debray predicts that this same superiority will be reduced since "there are already more Indian and Chinese engineers than there are American engineers". He describes the West as an "oligarch's club" which violates "the international charters which it would have non-natives follow to the letter". The West wants to make them happy "with guided missiles without them knowing anything about their history, their geography, their language, their religion and their customs...". For him, Europe is "a Spanish inn, where the English language rules, which has been entirely given over to market forces, and what remains of public authority is under the thumb of private financial empires and greedy lobbies" who have transformed a once beautiful dream into a "machine used to disarm, disempower, de-industrialize, dismember, and lobotomize".

For Renaud Girard, the warrior West forgets its defeats. It confuses a desire to promote democracy, justice, the respect for human rights everywhere with the right of interference that was invented by Jean-François Revel, theorized by Bernard Kouchner, taken up by Bernard-Henri Levy [all French] and modernized under the banner of humanitarian intervention and the responsibility to protect. A tragic example is Afghanistan where the promised democratization has turned into "corruption, opium trafficking, and general instability" [and finally the defeat of the Americans and victory for the Taliban].

Renaud Girard evokes the scourge of the "short-term", "the tyranny of public opinion", "the Hollywoodization of information" which appeared during the first Gulf War with the choice to summarize complex conflicts in two minutes on television. "Manicheism, an infantile disease of modern Western media is responsible for the blindness of most of the reporters who covered the Arab Spring."

"The bad is the one wielding the power and the good guy is the one on the street. Get rid of the former and everything will be fine." He is reminding us not to mistake our enemy. Thus, "Russian and Chinese nationalisms are not, at their core, fundamentally anti-Western." For Girard, the West should never abandon a diplomatic battleground until it has found a certain outcome. Finally, Girard praises the European Union, regretting its "operational paralysis and the growing disaffection of its constituents", and he concedes that the West has "shown itself to be clumsy, even irresponsible towards the other people of the world". We can accept this criticism.

Since the publication of my books *Uyghurs: Putting an End to the Fake News* and *China without Blinkers* (a book written by 17 intellectuals from 5 continents and published in July 2021 on the anniversary of the founding of the Communist Party of China) which I co-edited with Jean-Pierre Page, former head of international department at the Confédération Générale du Travail (CGT), I have given numerous interviews to Chinese newspapers, radio stations and television channels. Often, in fact almost always, my interviewers ask "What is the reason for this hostility, this aggressiveness on the part of the French media against China?" This is a question that has always puzzled me as the answer has always seemed obvious to me. The answer is that there is an all-out offensive being launched by the United States of America, a nation which rightly fears that its unchallenged reign as the single superpower has come to an end.

We must not forget one thing. In the first decades of its existence, the United States of America experienced war on its soil. It was the Civil War. Apart from the Civil War which lasted for four years, ending in 1865, the United States of America has never known a war against a foreign aggressor on its own soil — a rare and perhaps unique phenomenon among great countries. They have never had to face an invasion on their territory by an enemy army. None of their cities, roads, bridges, factories, hospitals and schools have been destroyed by aerial bombardment or cannon fire. They have never seen hordes of foreign soldiers invading their towns and villages, destroying, burning, robbing, massacring men, women, children and even infants, as they themselves did for example in Mỹ Lai in Vietnam where they murdered between 347 and 504 civilians on March 16, 1968, raping village women in groups before mutilating and killing them. The most cruel attack they have known was the destruction of the Twin Towers on September 11, 2001. It caused the death of 2,996 people. Of course, such death is deplorable, and caused by a terrorist attack. However, that should not prevent us from seeing that, since its creation, the United States of America has massacred millions of innocent people far from its own shores. They have been in a constant state of war, most often, against distant, weak countries, incapable of retaliating on American soil. Many of these countries were destroyed by the United States army, which allowed the looting of wealth and the monopolization of natural resources with the bonus of installing of dictators, puppets loyal to the victor. Here I will say, and I do not wish to sound macabre, that when we talk about September 11, everyone feels sorry, as they should, for the destruction of the Twin Towers, but sadly we almost always forget, another September 11, that of 1973, which saw the Chilean army led by General Augusto Pinochet rise up against its democratically elected government, bombing the presidential palace which housed President Salvador Allende before he committed suicide. This putsch was orchestrated, as it almost always is in that region of the world, by the CIA, the secret arm through which the United States carries out its dirty work. It is estimated that more than 3,000 Chileans died in the coup. Nearly 150,000 people were imprisoned for political reasons, nearly 27,000 were tortured and there were hundreds of thousands of political exiles. The strength of the US propaganda lies in the fact that it is able to succeed in erasing all these victims from memory, by highlighting the 2,996 victims of Twin Towers attack for whom we are invited to shed, on each anniversary date, tears of pity — for the so cruelly bruised "greatest democracy in the world".

In 2005 I co-wrote an essay titled *The United States, From Bad to Worse*. With my co-authors, I wanted to list the wars waged by the United States. We thought we could devote an entire book to reporting on these wars in detail. We therefore chose to only provide the location, the date, and the nature of each attack by the United States army. For example, for an aggression suffered by China we would simply write "China 1922-1927. Deployment or marine troops during nationalist revolts". Despite such stylistic brevity, our list of all the United States' military interventions between 1890 and 2003 still took up 6 pages.[16]

While in France, journalist Zheng Ruolin, the correspondent for several Chinese newspapers in Paris, published a delicious and mischievous book with the publisher Denoël titled *Chinese Are Men like the Other Men*. We should note why exactly this title is so incisive. Zheng indicates, because it is not obvious to all French people, that the Chinese are fellow humans. Our great national poet, Victor Hugo, the very man who so beautifully castigated the looting of the Yuanmingyuan Imperial Garden (the Old Summer Palace) in Peking by English and French thugs, exclaimed one day: "Ah, a fool is he that thinks that I am not you."

---

16. See Appendix 2

Zheng Ruolin is a warm man, full of humor, who loves France and his country alike. It is because he wanted Beijing and Paris to know and understand each other better that he wrote this book of love and peace, a didactic book. The author tells us about China and France, two countries (which he knows very well) which, for him, are destined to evolve, yet are sometimes jealous of each other. Here is what the back cover of his book says:

"China is developing at a breakneck speed. It sometimes provokes interest, arouses admiration and even frightens others, but it always intrigues others. What does the incredible transformation of the former Middle Kingdom mean for its 1,300 million people? In Beijing and Shanghai, as in the countryside, what are their joys, their frustrations or their hopes? For once, it's not a Westerner who is telling us what the Chinese think, fear, desire, consume... in short, how the Chinese live, work and have fun. Without jargon, but not without humour, and avoiding cliché, Zheng Ruolin addresses all aspects of the everyday life and concerns of the Chinese people. He does this so that we will know what the 500 million Internet users in the country are saying and telling each other, what the new "middle class" dream is about, how lovers in Guangdong or elsewhere behave, what it means to own a house or a car. It is an unusual portrait of the inhabitants of the future world's leading economic power, as it was seen, through the eyes of a child, by the author."

In this book, the author enlightens us and helps us to better understand China, and France too. He persuades us of the need to talk to each other more, in a way which befits two great powers that are not enemies, without fear or arrogance, and with mutual respect. There is a saying that goes, "When Peter tells me about Paul I learn more about Peter than about Paul." When I read sinophobic articles, I learn more about the journalists who wrote them than I do about China.

Just as President Xi Jinping said, to build a community with a shared future, the old zero-sum mentality must give way to win-win cooperation. Including, of course, the field of culture.

China first awoke, as I said, by tearing itself away from misery, poverty, technical underdevelopment and by putting in place, through the political system it chose under the leadership of the Communist Party of China, all the necessary conditions for its progress to continue and even accelerate, despite all the sometimes internal, but often external difficulties. Therefore, China no longer intends to suffer lessons, reprimands and threats, without responding to them, which is relatively new in political and diplomatic discussions with other countries and in particular Western countries. For example, Chinese ambassador to France, Mr. Lu Shaye, voices China's protests against lies and unfounded accusations. He does so with enough force to surprise our media and the French authorities, who felt it necessary to summon him to ask him for an explanation. I read Ambassador Zhang Jun's remarks at the Interactive Dialogue Between the Third Committee and the Special Rapporteur on Minority Issues at the UN on October 21, 2021.[17]

He quite forcefully condemned the United States, France and a few other countries that "cannot resist their bad habit" to "make grounless accusations against China, spread political virus and disinformation, and poison the atmosphere of cooperation", using "human rights as a pretext for political maneuvering". He then warns, "Your days of bullying and oppressing developing countries are long gone."

And, he counters by saying to the United States and a few other countries, "Your desperate attempts to cover up your own terrible human rights record will not work. The world sees it clearly. The US conducted genocide against the American Indians. It suppressed its own people to the point they yell 'I can't breathe'. It ignored the deaths of over 700,000 nationals due to the pandemic. And it stained its hands with the blood of hundreds of thousands of Muslim civilians in the Middle East and Central Asia. The list goes on. Human rights are not your

---

17. See https://www.fmprc.gov.cn/ce/ceun/eng/chinaandun/socialhr/3rdcommittee/ t1916019.htm and https://www.legrandsoir.info/chine-les-propos-stupefiants-de-l-ambassadeur-zhang-jun-sur-l-occident.html

cover-up. Blaming other countries will not wipe off your own misdeeds, but only reveal your evil and hypocrisy."

He again says to the United States and a few other countries, "Your attempts to get rid of those who hold different views in the name of democracy will only end in vain. Democracy is not your privilege, but a right enjoyed by peoples of all countries. The best democracy is to let people be the real master of the country, instead of making them the cannon fodder in political manipulation. The world is diverse. So are the approaches to realize democracy. Whether a country is democratic or not should be judged by its own people, not some individuals outside the country, let alone countries like you. Tragedies in countries such as Afghanistan, Iraq and Libya have proven time and again that military intervention from the outside and the so-called democratic transformation entail nothing but harm to those countries affected, and to the ideal of democracy itself."

Addressing France and other supporters of the United States, Zhang observed, "What you are doing is submitting your independence and autonomy, and serving as the henchmen of the US, as if you can gain superiority by acting at the beck and call of the superpower. But the truth is, you are giving up your own dignity, and will win no respect from others." [18]

---

18. See https://www.mfa.gov.cn/ce/ceun/eng/dbtxx/czdbzjds/zjdshd/t1916019.htm

# Conclusion

I would like to conclude this text by returning to what I wrote at the beginning. As I said my Chinese friends, mainly journalists, often ask me, "What is the reason for this hostility, this aggressiveness on the part of the French media against China?" This is a question that has always puzzled me as the answer has always seemed obvious. The answer is of course that there is an all-out offensive being launched by the United States of America against China, because it rightly fears that its unchallenged reign as a single superpower has come to an end.

It is important to mention here (and when you think about it, it seems logical) that this aggressiveness from the French media against China, or this hostility, manifests itself in the same way and with as much aggressiveness against all those (politicians, writers, journalists) whose remarks, analyses and testimonies in any way somehow deny or thwart the huge campaign of fake news from the United States of America aimed at China. We are in the midst of a real war of ideas, and an ideological battle with no room for concessions, that tolerates no weakness, and which is devoid of morality. Here I refer not to things that have been passed on to me, but to things that I have experienced personally and sometimes with a violence that I did believe should be the subject of. It is true that the only weapon is my pen. I am not part of any governing body. I am not in a position to make concrete decisions that could affect the United States and the Western camp in its fight against the "irremediable" evil that the West can see in the rise of power from China.

In any case, as I have shown in the report by the French Army's Strategic Research Institute (IRSEM), in which my name is echoed, and the allies of the United States of America do not accept that there could be any space for free expression, any place of truth in which the lies against China can be revealed. This is the reason why they harassed me, your humble author. This is why the media threw themselves at me with slander and insults.

For a long time I had a literary agent to whom I had entrusted the task of proposing the manuscripts of my novels to major publishers. She knew them well. Sometimes she telephoned me at the end of the week to tell me that certain publishers had accepted one of my manuscripts. A few days later she phoned me again to tell me that after thinking it over, the publisher no longer wanted it. She would add, "Stop with politics." I told you above how I gave up contacting the big publishers. In the case of my book, *Uyghurs: Putting an End to the Fake News*, I knew as I wrote it that finding a publisher would not be easy. The book was nevertheless published by a publishing house owned by a French intellectual, Sonia Bressler, who knew Xinjiang. She and I suffered enough attacks to make us think twice about repeating such "brazen" act, enough attacks to discourage other writers or intellectuals from imitating us. Someone said that the first casualty of a war is always the truth. This can also be said of the battle of ideas. Those who have not experienced this cannot imagine to what extent our opponents consider us as enemies. A few years ago, because of a dispute over Syria, a journalist from a satirical weekly (*Charlie-Hebdo*) informed me on the telephone that he had launched an investigation into me, "with colleagues including the editor, with colleagues from other newspapers and even with foreign colleagues". More than ten years later, I'm still waiting. A journalist from the *Liberation* searched my publisher's accounts in the hope of discovering sums of dubious origin. Were they looking for RMB? The authors of the report "China Influences Operations: A Machiavellian Moment" went digging into my past as far back as the 1960s. They are welcome to look into my life as a committed journalist, and a writer. They will find nothing that can harm me, nothing that can undermine my honor or my respectability.

If an explanation had to be found for such attacks, without attributing to any extraordinary or superhuman powers, that is, without being immodest, we would do well to remind ourselves of the words of our friend Antonio Gramsci: "Only the truth is revolutionary."

# Appendix 1

To respond to the calumnies on China, working together with Jean-Pierre Page (former head of the international department of the CGT, former literary referent of ATTAC), I brought together 17 intellectuals from five continents to write a book which was published in July 2021 for the 100th anniversary of the founding of the Communist Party of China. We titled it: *China without Blinkers.* The authors include a journalist, a writer, a professor, a university doctor, an essayist, an economist, a student, a researcher in philosophy, a member of the CNRS (short for Centre national de la recherche scientifique), a former ambassador, a collaborator at the UN, a deputy director of the institute for research on world development, an attaché to a ministry of foreign affairs, a radio host, and a TV host.

Then, still to broaden the protest internationally, Jean-Pierre Page, and Aymeric Monville, our publisher, launched a petition to demand the right to talk about China in a new way, that is to say, the right not to be forced to write systematically against China, not to speak only of its faults (it does have some), but to be allowed to write of its successes and qualities. The text of the petition was first entrusted to a platform, a French subsidiary of Change.Org. However, very quickly, an order was given from the United States to censor it. We had to find another platform ("My opinions.com"). I present the text of the petition for the right to speak differently about China here.

## Petition

We claim the right to speak otherwise of China.

In France we saw a man given a real drubbing. That man was Maxime Vivas, a French writer who has visited Xinjiang twice and published a book in December 2020 (*Uyghurs: Putting an End to the Fake News*, Silk Road editions) and has since co-edited with Jean-Pierre Page *China without Blinkers* (July 2021, Delga editions) written by 17 intellectuals from five continents.

We have seen an avalanche of insults and calumnies fall on Maxime Vivas, "useful idiot, fool, anomaly, absurd author, extremist, conspirator, penholder and parrot of the Chinese, bought by China, propaganda amplifier for the Chinese, fanciful, founder of a site that publishes far-right articles" and, finally, the coup de grace by the process of "reductio ad hitlerum", the idea that Vivas is "red-brown", that is to say a Nazi, when in truth he has written four anti-fascist books and he is from an anti-Franco Spanish family.

What is remarkable, in this circus where public and private media (France Inter, Radio France International, *Liberation, Le Monde*, l'Obs, Stop on Images, Le Canard enchaîné, TMC-TF1, Charlie Hebdo) prance around is that the ad hominem attacks mask the non-existence of criticism of the actual content of his books.

What our media do not support is quite simply the publication of non-Sinophobic, non-racist works, which do not support imperialist wars. One does not have to be considered pro-Chinese to have the dogs unleash on them, and it is enough that he is suspected of being pro-truth. Vivas is guilty of existing, no matter what he writes. Thus, the recent report by the IRSEM (Institut de Recherche Stratégique de l'Ecole Militaire), a para-public organization dependent on the Ministry of the Armed Forces, whose violent partisan remarks are matched only by deliberate untruths and inaccuracies, quotes Maxime Vivas fifty-four times in his six hundred and fifty-four pages, designating him as a "Chinese agent".

These infamous and slanderous attacks contravene the requirements of the Journalists' Charter. They are attacks on the freedom of expression. They harm the image of journalism. They recall ancient times, when certain penholders in the service of an occupier wallowed cowardly in collaboration. This kind of journalism which smacks of the 1930s anti-semitic weekly, "I am everywhere", only follows what is dictated by the dominant thought and the principals of an oligarchy, and that is the problem. This press has renounced any real critical spirit and therefore its independence. Paul Nizan stigmatized the press as "guard dogs". Today newsrooms are populated by small talentless mercenaries where they distill their gall in the service of the powerful.

With the signatories below including the authors of the book *China without Blinkers* (a journalist, a writer, a professor, a university doctor, an essayist, an economist, a student, a researcher in philosophy, a member of the CNRS, a former ambassador, a collaborator at the UN, a deputy director of the institute for research on world development, an attaché to a ministry of foreign affairs, a radio host, and a TV host), to all those speaking about China from Europe, to Asia, to Africa, to Latin America, and Oceania, we demand that this veritable manhunt cease and that the war drums of imperialism be silenced, as they would lead us, according to the new military doctrine of the French General Staff, towards a "high intensity conflict". Let's respect China as it respects us![19]

---

**19**. See https://www.mesopinions.com/petition/politique/halte-demonisation-chine/161942

# Appendix 2

## A partial list of U.S. military interventions since 1890[20]

The list does not include: compulsory presence of the military police during demonstrations; mobilizations of the National Guard; offshore shows of naval strength; reinforcement of the embassy staff; the use of non-Defense Department personnel (such as the Drug Enforcement Administration); military exercises; non-combat mobilizations; the permanent stations of armed forces; covert actions where the United States did not play a command and control role; the majority of troop interventions; piloting of foreign aircraft by Americans; foreign disaster assistance; military training and advisory programs not involving direct combat; civic action programs and many other military activities; the use of

---

**20**. Primary Sources: *Congressional Record* (June 23, 1969), 180 Landings by the U.S. Marine Corp History Division, Ege & Makhijani in Counterspy (July-August 1982), and Daniel Ellsberg in *Protest & Survive*. "Instances of Use of United States Forces Abroad, 1798-1993" by Ellen C. Collier of the Library of Congress Congressional Research Service. Compiled by Zoltan Grossman, 1705 Rutledge, Madison, WI 53704 Phone/Fax (608)246-2256.

mercenaries[21] and armies of third countries (Israel, Saudi Arabia...) to fight in their place, or the creation of "color revolutions" allowing an armed force of the United States (NATO) to provoke wars such as the Russia's current conflict with Ukraine in 2022.

| Location | Date |
| --- | --- |
| Argentina | 1890 |
| Chile | 1891 |
| Haiti | 1891 |
| Hawaii | 1893 |
| Nicaragua | 1894 |
| China | 1894-1895 |
| Korea | 1894-1896 |
| Panama | 1895 |
| Nicaragua | 1896 |
| China | 1898-1900 |
| Philippines | 1899-1913 |
| Cuba | 1898 |
| Puerto Rico | 1898 |

---

21. Sean McFate, former US Army officer: "We see mercenaries all over the world, in Yemen, Somalia, Iraq, Syria, Ukraine, Congo and Venezuela. Many of them started out on contracts with the US government in countries like Iraq [⋯]. Americans do not fuss over contractor casualties, unlike dead marines."
http://www.slate.fr/story/186833/guerres-mercenaires-soldats-americains-donald-trump-syrie-irak-afghanistan-blackwater-wagner

| | |
|---|---|
| Nicaragua | 1898 |
| Samoa | 1898 |
| Nicaragua | 1899 |
| Panama | 1901-1914 |
| Panama | 1903 |
| Honduras | 1903 |
| The Dominican Republic | 1903-1904 |
| Korea | 1904-1905 |
| Cuba | 1906-1909 |
| Nicaragua | 1907 |
| Honduras | 1907 |
| Panama | 1908 |
| Nicaragua | 1910 |
| Honduras | 1911 |
| China | 1911 |
| Cuba | 1912 |
| Panama | 1912 |
| Honduras | 1912 |
| Nicaragua | 1912-1933 |
| Mexico | 1913 |
| The Dominican Republic | 1914 |
| Mexico | 1914-1918 |
| Haiti | 1914-1934 |
| The Dominican Republic | 1916-1924 |
| Cuba | 1917-1933 |

| World War I | 1917-1918 |
|---|---|
| Soviet Russia | 1918-1922 |
| Panama | 1918-1920 |
| Yugoslavia | 1919 |
| Honduras | 1919 |
| Guatemala | 1920 |
| Turkey | 1922 |
| China | 1922-1927 |
| Honduras | 1924-25 |
| Panama | 1925 |
| China | 1927-1934 |
| World War II | 1941-1945 |
| Iran | 1946 |
| Yugoslavia | 1946 |
| Uruguay | 1947 |
| Greece | 1947-1949 |
| China | 1948-1949 |
| Germany | 1948 |
| Philippines | 1948-1954 |
| Puerto Rico | 1950 |
| Korean War | 1950-1953 |
| Iran | 1953 |
| Vietnam | 1954 |
| Guatemala | 1954 |

| | |
|---|---|
| Egypt | 1956 |
| Lebanon | 1958 |
| Iraq | 1958 |
| China | 1958 |
| Panama | 1958 |
| Vietnam | 1960-1975 |
| Cuba | 1961 |
| Germany | 1961 |
| Cuba | 1962 |
| Laos | 1962 |
| Cuba | 1962-(le blocus toujours en vigueur à ce jour) |
| Panama | 1964 |
| Indonesia | 1965 |
| The Dominican Republic | 1965-1966 |
| Guatemala | 1966-1967 |
| Cambodia | 1969-1975 |
| Oman | 1970 |
| Laos | 1971-1973 |
| The Middle East | 1973 |
| Chile | 1973 |
| Cambodia | 1975 |
| Angola | 1976-1992 |
| Iran | 1980 |

| Libya | 1981 |
|---|---|
| El Salvador | 1981-1992 |
| Nicaragua | 1981-1990 |
| Lebanon | 1982-1984 |
| Honduras | 1983-1989 |
| Grenade | 1983-1984 |
| Iran | 1984 |
| Libya | 1986 |
| Bolivia | 1986 |
| Iran | 1987-1988 |
| Libya | 1989 |
| BVI (British Virgin Islands) | 1989 |
| Philippines | 1989 |
| Panama | 1989-1990 |
| Liberia | 1990 |
| Saudi Arabia | 1990-1991 |
| Iraq | 1990-1991 |
| Kuwait | 1991 |
| Somalia | 1992-1994 |
| Yugoslavia | 1992-1994 |
| Bosnia | 1993-1995 |
| Haiti | 1994-1996 |
| Zaïre (Congo) | 1996-1997 |
| Liberia | 1997 |

| Albania | 1997 |
|---|---|
| Sudan | 1998 |
| Afghanistan | 1998 |
| Yugoslavia | 1999 |
| Yemen | 2000 |
| Macedonia | 2001 |
| United States | 2001 |
| Afghanistan | 2001-2022 |
| Iraq | 2003-2021 |

* The dates haven' t been got the consensus among the different historians. They are given by historians based on their political views.

Excerpt is taken from the book *Les Etats-Unis de mal empire* (Aden Belgium edition) that I wrote with Danielle Bleitrach and Viktor Dedaj. The list of American wars in the book (published in 2005) does not extend beyond the year 2003. To that list we can now add the wars in Libya (2011-2019) and Syria (2014-2019). It would not be too bold to state that the United States is waging a war on Russia today, through its proxy, Ukraine.

# About the Author

Maxime Vivas has written 24 books of various kinds, including novels, detective stories, essays, humorous stories and youth novels, etc.

His works have been translated into 13 languages: English, Spanish, Chinese (simplified Chinese), Chinese (Tibetan), Chinese (Uighur), Turkish, Portuguese, German, Italian, Arabic, Japanese, Korean and Esperanto. The first translated work can be traced back to 2005.

He has won three awards: the first one was in 1997; and the recent one was in 2021, which was "the 15th Special Book Award of China". In 2008, he was nominated for the "Interpretation of Politics" Prize.

Among his 24 books, six are in the collection of Library of Congress in the United States, which has some restrictions on book borrowing (books there are mainly accessible to senior government officials)[22].

Over the past twenty years and more, he has compered the one-hour cultural live program at Mon Païs (My Kingdom of Broadcast) every Monday in Toulouse, France.

Since 2008, he has been the website administrator of "Le Grand Soir". Due to the political inclination of his website "Le Grand Soir", he has been slandered and threatened, and suffered from infiltration and accusation.

---

22. See https://id.loc.gov/rwo/agents/n99032025.html

www.ingramcontent.com/pod-product-compliance
Lightning Source LLC
Chambersburg PA
CBHW051432270326
41934CB00019B/3486